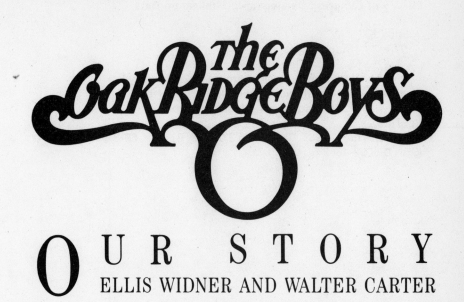

OUR STORY

ELLIS WIDNER AND WALTER CARTER

CONTEMPORARY
BOOKS, INC.
CHICAGO ▪ NEW YORK

Library of Congress Cataloging-in-Publication Data

Widner, Ellis.
    The Oak Ridge Boys.

    1. Oak Ridge Boys (Musical group)   2. Country
musicians—United States—Biography.   I. Carter,
Walter.   II. Oak Ridge Boys (Musical group)
III. Title.
ML421.O2W5   1987   784.5′2′00922 [B]   86-31914
ISBN 0-8092-4842-5

For additional information regarding all photograph copyrights,
contact The Oak Ridge Boys, Inc., 329 Rockland Road,
Hendersonville, TN 37075.

Published by Contemporary Books, Inc.
180 North Michigan Avenue, Chicago, Illinois 60601
Manufactured in the United States of America
Library of Congress Catalog Card Number: 86-31914
International Standard Book Number: 0-8092-4842-5

Published simultaneously in Canada by Beaverbooks, Ltd.
195 Allstate Parkway, Valleywood Business Park
Markham, Ontario L3R 4T8 Canada

CONTENTS

PREFACE

Everybody has his own story.—Bob Weber, Oak
Ridge Quartet bass singer, 1949–1956.

I was a good thousand miles from home, on a
minor league baseball diamond in Fort Lauderdale, Florida, standing in the dirt around home
plate, looking at the back of a man whose
friends called him "Preacher," banging away for all I
was worth on an acoustic guitar while Preacher and
his three buddies complained ironically in song, "Nobody wants to play rhythm guitar behind Jesus."

How did I get here? That was easy. I had been out
drinking the night before with Jimbeau Hinson (co-
writer of "I'm Settin' Fancy Free") in Hendersonville, Tennessee. At or about midnight, someone
helped us—rolled us, actually—up the steps onto a
tour bus to face a sobering situation. The bus had
maybe eight bunks, and by the next morning it would
be carrying four gospel singers, a four-piece band, a
sound man, a driver, two secretaries, and a guy we
picked up in Atlanta who, for reasons known only to
him, wanted to manage this menagerie. Plus two
songwriters.

That's how *I* got here. The question is how *they* got here. They were, after all, The Oak Ridge Boys. They were supposed to be one of the biggest acts in gospel music, and here they were, riding to the gig in somebody else's too-small bus because they had had to lease theirs out to rock stars to make some money to pay the repair bill. Here they were, even the singers—the stars—hauling equipment, setting up their own amps and sound system, running to the bus to change clothes for the show, then changing back to load everything on the bus again. Here they were, sleeping on the bus, bargaining with motels for a day rate on two rooms with extra towels so they could at least shower before a show. And here they were at the "show," gospel headliners opening for the Key West Cubs and the Fort Lauderdale Expos.

When I thought about it, it didn't seem any more unlikely than the circumstances under which I first became associated with The Oak Ridge Boys five years earlier, in late 1971. I was playing a writers' night at Nashville's Exit/In, and a songwriter named Jack Ross introduced himself and asked me if I ever wrote any gospel songs.

No, I never had. Never had even thought about it. Then he asked me if I was familiar with The Oak Ridge Boys. Same answer. (Ironically, if I had been pressed to name a gospel artist, I would have dredged up a childhood memory from TV ads of the fifties— Wally Fowler, founder of the Oak Ridge Quartet.)

The Oaks were a pretty big gospel group, Jack explained, and their drummer, Mark Ellerbee, was looking for material for a solo album—not the heavy-duty washed-in-the-blood stuff, but "contemporary" or "message" music, light on the gospel and heavy on the beat.

I didn't know the first thing about gospel, but I had just turned twenty-one, just graduated from college, and just arrived in Nashville to show Kristofferson a thing or two about songwriting. I could write you a gospel song, by God, or any other kind of song you wanted.

I wrote one the next day called "Happy Man" and took it to Silverline Music, the Oaks' publishing company. Over the next few years I wrote some more, and we did demonstration tapes of several of them, but despite my gospel efforts, the Oaks more often than not would rather hear me sing songs like "God Gets the Women," "Green Stamp for the Lord," and "Do You Still Love Me, or What?" The sacrilegious stuff made them a little nervous during thunderstorms, but I don't think they ever blamed me for their hard times.

By the time I went to Florida with them, I was a staff writer drawing—*draining*, actually—$75 a week from Silverline. Around the end of 1975, I had my first song recorded when the Oaks did "Last Train to Glory." Appropriate to my first introduction to them, Mark Ellerbee sang the lead vocal. The Oaks started singing it on their live show—at least when I was out with them they did.

In the meantime, I went into the studio (Duane's studio) with Joe Sun, who was then a country promotion man, and recorded a purposely god-awful version of "Or What?" The Oaks not only sang backup on my record, putting me in such exalted company as Jimmy Buffett and Paul Simon; they did it for free.

In addition to my songwriter's draw, I was working as a bartender, so I had plenty of money and I was having lots of fun. The Oaks, however, were not having much of either. If they had had a little less determination and a little more business sense, they would have quit. But Bill Golden and Duane Allen (Richard and Joe were not yet partners) were two of the most determined men I have ever known—Bill determined to bust the Oaks loose from the trappings of gospel music no matter what, Duane to keep them alive no matter what.

Jim Halsey (the group's longtime co-manager and

booking agent) booked the baseball date, and he
would eventually book the group back into solvency
(an understatement). But in early 1976, they needed
to trim away any unnecessary expenses, and I was
one of those. I hated to lose the gig, but I couldn't in
good conscience argue.

I had little contact with the Oaks for the next two
years, during which time they sold the publishing
companies to Halsey and I went to work for *The
Tennessean*, Nashville's morning newspaper. But in
1982, after four-and-a-half frustrating years of *cover-
ing* success stories (including the Oaks) rather than
being one, I wanted to write songs again. The Oaks
had bought the company back from Halsey and hired
Noel Fox, a former Oak and a man who liked beer as
much as I did, to run the company. I quit the paper
and became a Silverline writer again. It was like
coming home.

Three years later, the Oaks had cut two more of my
songs and William Lee Golden was putting a third
one on his solo album, but it was time to leave home.
Again, there were no hard feelings, but this time
there was no steady job to fall back on.

I told Duane there ought to be a book written about
the Oaks and that I ought to do it. As it happened,
Ellis Widner proposed a book project at the same
time, and that's the main reason we ended up doing it
together.

On February 12, 1986, I climbed (unassisted this
time) onto the bus with the Oaks and started the tape
recorder. William Lee spoke first: "What you ought
to write is *The Mystery History of The Oak Ridge
Boys*."

That's how it started. I don't know if we solved any
great mysteries, but thanks to the openness and
cooperation of the Oaks and their entire organization,
we uncovered some new and interesting things about
The Oak Ridge Boys, both present and past.

Mine is not the only story, of course. Ellis has a story. As a reporter for *The Tulsa Tribune* (Tulsa is the home base of the Jim Halsey Company), he first saw The Oak Ridge Boys when they were still gospel. In 1977, he became one of the first journalists to review them as a country act. Later he saw their showcase during deejay week in Nashville (the same event at which they had first met Halsey three years earlier) and interviewed them for the first of many times to come.

As I discovered when digging through the Oaks' files, Ellis also started laying the groundwork for a book deal back then, with a letter to the Oaks thanking them and suggesting they talk at greater length sometime in the future. Through the years, they talked many times. Ellis went out on the road with them, an experience he wrote about in *Billboard*, and got to know and understand them as well as or better than any reporter in the business.

There are four stories—William Lee, Duane, Richard, and Joe—that together are, of course, the reason for this book. But there are also forty-odd former members of The Oak Ridge Boys and the Oak Ridge Quartet, all of whom have stories that are well worth the telling. At a photo session that included some former and present group members, William Lee pointed to his predecessors and said, "Those guys, they're the ones. They're the reason we can do what we do today."

Almost every singer whose name appears in this book took the time to answer all the questions I could think of and then patiently explained and reexplained until I understood. Their memories were fascinating as well as invaluable, and it is with deep, deep regret that their stories have been for the most part cut down to a few paragraphs.

I'm also indebted to Christie Hudson, who literally kept me alive with food, drink, and moral support through the long weeks while the check was in the mail.

Walter Carter
Nashville, Tennessee, August 1, 1986

Who?

Jim Halsey was, in his usual easy-talking but firm and persuasive manner, trying to convince me that I really needed to see the new group he had recently signed.

It was the first time The Oak Ridge Boys had come to Tulsa, and it was a performance I've never forgotten. I had just started writing reviews as a correspondent for *The Tulsa Tribune*. The show still had mostly gospel songs in it, but there was a magic—an energy—that transcended musical barriers.

Halsey calls them "pure entertainment." That's about the best—and most accurate—description you could ask for.

In the ten years since, the Oaks have consistently outdone themselves. Even on an off night, they were better than most so-called entertainers on a good night and could knock an audience dead, sending a reviewer scrambling for a thesaurus.

I got my first baptism in touring with the Oaks on a bus ride through Kansas and Oklahoma in 1978. It was an eye-opening experience that became a two-page feature for *Billboard*. I was bone-tired after it was over, yet exhilarated.

The Oaks and I have talked many times over the years since, and I've always appreciated their openness, honesty, and constructive criticism. They're a lot of fun, too.

I ran into Walter Carter several times over the years while he was working for *The Tennessean* and I was in Nashville for *The Tulsa Tribune*. We got better acquainted through our mutual friend Debbie

Banks. In writing this book with him, I've learned a lot about the Oaks and the incredible sense of history the group represents. Thanks to Walter, I've also found a couple of new watering holes in Music City.

Here's to more . . . books and watering holes.

When you undertake a project such as this, there are people who make your job easier and possible. First, of course, the Oaks themselves and their staff, particularly Kathy Harris. They made it possible for *my* dream to come true—writing this book. And Jim Halsey, for introducing his "new act" to me. Kathy Gangwisch, the Oaks' publicist, offered moral support, countless press clippings and insights. Leo Zabelin has been around the Oaks for years, and his viewpoints and encouragement were more valuable to me than he realizes.

The long hours of writing and researching are made easier when you have the help and support of your friends. Without Phil Pruitt and Mary Hargrove, my life would be a lot emptier. And, what self-respecting son wouldn't thank his mother? It was her and my father's love of country music that helped inspire mine.

It is to them I dedicate my efforts.

Ellis Widner
Tulsa, Oklahoma, August 1, 1986

1
"THREE MINUTES AWAY ..."

You are three minutes away from stardom."
That's what Jim Halsey kept telling The
Oak Ridge Boys. Three minutes—the length
of a hit record.

Halsey, their booking agent and eventually their
manager, had had this three-minute business on his
mind ever since the first show the Oaks worked for
him. That was in 1975 in Warwick, Rhode Island, as
a fill-in for Roy Clark. Sometime between the soundcheck and the actual show, Duane was hanging
around the stage, and Halsey started talking business.

That was a shock in itself. Halsey had met them the
previous fall, backstage at the Opry House after their
showcase for the annual country disc jockey convention. He had been complimentary then and cordial in
their few conversations thereafter, but he had *never*
talked business. This was, after all, the Oaks' first
date with him, and they hadn't even gone onstage yet.
They didn't have any working agreement, verbal or

otherwise. Nevertheless, he told Duane of his plans for The Oak Ridge Boys.

"I'm going to put you in Vegas until we have time to get you off the label you're on," Halsey said. "Then, if we can get a *three-minute hit* . . ."

Duane was a disc jockey before he was a professional singer. He already knew the value of a three-minute hit. When he joined The Oak Ridge Boys in 1966, his first action was to take every extra copy he could find of their new single, "Less of Me," and, even though it featured his predecessor on the lead part, send it off to every country radio station in the Northeast. He *knew* the difference three minutes can make in a career.

He also knew how many long years that three-minute dream can stretch into. And by the middle of 1976—a year after the Rhode Island show—Halsey's three minutes seemed more like three light-years to The Oak Ridge Boys. If it seemed they were three minutes away from anything, it was oblivion.

Joe Bonsall, tenor, had been with the Oaks less than three years. The youngest and the most outwardly energetic of the four singers, Joe was worried. When he joined the Oaks, they were sitting on top of the gospel music world. And Joe was sitting on top of his own world, too—the father of a new baby girl.

Suddenly, it seemed, The Oak Ridge Boys were pariahs. They could not get a gospel booking to save their professional lives. They were singing some kind of gospel-pop-country hybrid "message" music, leaning ever farther away from standard gospel lyrics. Gospel music had saved Joe from whatever future a member of a Philadelphia street gang might have, but the Oaks were leaving gospel music behind. He wondered, if the Oaks broke up, would the gospel fans—and more importantly, gospel acts and gospel promoters—be forgiving and take him back into the fold? He wondered if his wife would forgive him for singing those "secular" songs.

Richard Sterban, bass, had been with the Oaks only a year longer than Joe, and, like Joe, he was on a salary—a salary threatened by the lack of work and lack of hit records. When he joined the Oaks, he left a good job with the Stamps Quartet. They had backed up Elvis Presley in Las Vegas, and Richard had even been in a film, standing around a piano while Elvis played and led his own old-time gospel singing. When Richard left the Stamps, it was partly because deep down he had always felt a little uncomfortable in the glittery world of Elvis, Vegas, and pop music. But look at him now. The Oak Ridge Boys were playing Vegas, the same as Elvis had, but for nothing near the same money. He wondered if maybe he and Joe could start up their old group again, the Keystones, in the event the Oaks folded. Maybe it was time to get out of the singing business altogether. It sure wasn't helping his marriage, and it was keeping him away from his three young sons. He wondered if his speaking voice, which was as low and resonant as his singing voice, could get him a job as a sports announcer, maybe as a color commentator for Vanderbilt basketball games.

William Lee Golden, baritone, was at the lowest point of his life. His marriage, strained by his lifestyle on the road, had finally broken. One thing he did not worry about was money. He had none. He didn't even have a home. He was living in the Oaks' office. He had had big plans for The Oak Ridge Boys, even before he joined them in 1965. He had always been a dreamer and a pacesetter for the group, trying to keep them ahead of the crowd in every way from dress to music. He may have had the weakest singing voice in the group, but it had been the strongest when it came to pulling the Oaks out of gospel music and into something bigger and wider-reaching. The move from a small gospel label to the giant Columbia was the first step in that direction, but it was not working. In fact, it was a disaster.

More than anyone else, William Lee held on to his dreams for The Oak Ridge Boys. He had to. Dreams were all he had left to hold on to.

Duane Allen, lead singer, had been a gospel star almost from the day he joined The Oak Ridge Boys in 1966. His first album with the group was called *Duane Allen Out Front.* He had not only sung lead; he had also been the driving force behind the growth of the Oaks' business interests. He had taken over some of the group's management responsibilities from Golden while Golden tried to settle his personal life. Duane's marriage was solid, but how long could he support a wife and two small children on $200 a week? He had always thought of himself as a good businessman, but now he and William Lee were making less than anybody else in the group—*their* group. A few months earlier, he had thought the Oaks' financial problems could not get any worse. But they had. In a desperate attempt to make payroll and keep The Oak Ridge Boys together, he took money out of a withholding tax account. Now, in addition to losing all he had worked for, he could go to jail.

"Three minutes away," Halsey kept saying. It was the punch line of his pep talk every time the Oaks got discouraged at the thought of working harder and harder and not seeming to get anywhere. Halsey would talk about making progress and about having to make sacrifices to accomplish anything. And then he would always say, "We are three minutes away from stardom." Well, the Oaks had been around in one form or another for three *decades*, and the lessons of that history were not encouraging.

First of all, the Oaks had always been a brash, young, innovative bunch. The Oaks of 1976 were still innovative, still pretty brash, but they were not getting any younger. Only Joe was still in his twenties, and, unlike those other oaks—the trees—a thirty-year-old *singing* Oak had been a rare sight through the years.

The most depressing aspect of the Oaks' history was the fact that, despite their consistent notoriety, they had always been one of the most unstable acts in their field. The Oak Ridge Quartet, as the group had originally been known, was a star act on the Grand Ole Opry in the late forties, but four members got mad at their leader and quit in 1949. The replacement group became one of the top draws on the all-night singings in the early fifties, but they too disbanded in 1956. And the next group, the one that evolved into the current Oak Ridge Boys, fell on such hard times that they had to work straight jobs for a year and sing only on weekends.

The pattern of history showed boom times followed by disaster. The Oak Ridge Boys of 1976 had had their boom time at the top of gospel music. If the pattern ran true, the end was near.

And it did not appear that they could break the pattern by leaving gospel music for country. That too was a part of their history. They had started out as a country group back in 1945, but their audiences insisted on hearing gospel. Their lead singer in the mid-fifties quit gospel to pursue a career as a night-club singer, but he failed completely and was soon back in gospel.

The Oak Ridge Boys could possibly beg forgiveness—not from God but from the gospel music industry—for their sinful country ambitions and be welcomed back into the fold. After all, the legendary Blackwood Brothers had, only a few years earlier, so influenced the Dove Award voting that their slate of nominees swept every category (causing the awards to be invalidated that year), but all was forgiven once they publicly apologized.

That tactic might not work for The Oak Ridge Boys, however. Their innovative and progressive attitude had stretched the boundaries of gospel to the breaking point, and they had not left on friendly terms. The little wars that developed between them and the gospel hardliners were marked by some vicious public attacks from their fellow performers. And in the entire year of 1975, the major gospel promoters had booked them on a total of three dates (as opposed to the usual 150).

There was no looking back—much less turning back—now for The Oak Ridge Boys.

The road ahead into country music was not yet even a trail to follow. Billy Sherrill of Columbia Records, the Oaks' label, told them that he thought there was room for only one group in country music and that that group was not the Oaks but the Statlers, who had been firmly entrenched since the late sixties. (Like the Oaks, the Statlers started in gospel, but, unlike the Oaks, they never achieved any stature in the field and they downplayed that background whenever possible.)

Without the support of their own record label, the Oaks' faith in themselves wavered at times. But some people *did* believe in them. Johnny Cash had believed in them since 1971, when they played on his TV show. He had written a letter of recommendation to a Las Vegas hotel. He hired them himself in Vegas, overpaid them, and admonished them to stick together.

Jim Halsey also believed in them. And if Halsey could get the right people to see and listen, The Oak Ridge Boys could make believers out of them, too. After all, they were only three minutes away. If you don't believe it, just ask Jim Halsey.

In the early part of 1977, The Oak Ridge Boys gathered around four microphones in Nashville's Woodland Sound Studios, ready to record their first album for their new label, ABC Records. The tape rolled, the band played a few bars, and Duane started singing: "She played tambourine with a silver jingle. . . ."

It had taken years and years of hard work and no small amount of pain and suffering, but The Oak Ridge Boys were finally there, right where Jim Halsey insisted they were all along—just three minutes away, three minutes away from a hit record and a level of success they had not even dreamed about.

The word Oak Ridge *was pretty hot. It signified advanced technology, the atom bomb, the Manhattan Project. People had sort of gone nuts about it.—* Grant Turner, Grand Ole Opry announcer, 1944 to present

*The name might have something to do with the group. . . . They've always had a certain spark, even before I was with them. You could feel it, whatever it was. The members have completely changed over the years, but the spark is still there.—*Glen Allred, Oak Ridge Quartet guitarist, 1951-52

2
FROM LITTLE ACORNS

On January 1, 1943, there was no Oak Ridge—no town, no name, and no people. Only two months earlier the Army had designated 59,000 acres of land in a valley between the Cumberland and Smoky Mountain ranges, the center of which was about eighteen miles west of Knoxville, Tennessee, as the Kingston Demolition Range, and all 3,000 residents of settlements like Scarboro, Robertsville, and Wheat had been evacuated. A few construction workers had arrived on November 22, 1942, and at their suggestion the place was named Oak Ridge, after Black Oak Ridge, one of the five pine- and oak-covered ridges in the area.

Within two years, 75,000 people had moved there, and nobody—not even the majority of the new residents—knew why. But from the tight security at the guard gates, it was obvious the military was involved in a secret project.

It was a secret, all right—the best kept secret of World War II. It was the Manhattan Project. The atom bomb.

The mystique of the secret town was not lost on Wally Fowler, a young singer whose newly formed band, the Georgia Clodhoppers, had a regular spot on WNOX radio's "Mid-Day Merry Go Round" in Knoxville. The Clodhoppers were a hillbilly band, but they also sang gospel songs in a quartet style, and Fowler thought the quartet needed separate billing.

One day he was talking to a fellow WNOX musician, a skinny guitar player named Chet Atkins, who remembers Fowler saying, "You know, Oak Ridge is a new town, and this is a new group. That would be a good name."

On August 6, 1945, the first atom bomb exploded over Hiroshima. Likewise, the secrecy surrounding Oak Ridge exploded, and the town's notoriety grew as fast as the soon-to-be familiar mushroom cloud. The whole country was suddenly talking about a place that only days before did not officially exist.

Wally Fowler was always looking to exploit a current event (he had already recorded a song that played on the wartime word *propaganda*), and this current event ranked right up there with D-Day and Pearl Harbor.

Oak Ridge, he had said in an offhand remark, would be a good name. It was one of the biggest understatements and truest prophecies in the history of music. The group called "The Oak Ridge" has weathered more than forty years of ups and downs and more than forty personnel changes to emerge as one of the greatest success stories in the entertainment business.

It has been a good name, indeed.

The Oak Ridge Boys of today built their reputation on two basic elements—a progressive, innovative, and often controversial approach to music and an exciting live show. It is not just their trademark; it is part of a legacy that goes back even before Oak Ridge, to a group known as the John Daniel Quartet.

"Everything Wally did, he followed what John Daniel started," said Boyce Hawkins, pianist for Daniel and later for the Oak Ridge Quartet. "Wally magnified the showmanship part."

Daniel led the first full-time, professional gospel quartet. In 1935, he discovered John Wallace "Wally" Fowler, an eighteen-year-old singer from Rome, Georgia, and hired him to sing baritone and do comedy routines. Five years later, the John Daniel Quartet became the first gospel quartet to join the Grand Ole Opry. By the fall of 1943, Fowler was ready to apply the lessons of his eight-year apprenticeship to his own career. He left Daniel and moved to Knoxville, where he became a regular on WNOX radio.

In Oak Ridge, where no one was allowed to leave or even discuss his job among friends, the workers needed entertaining. The Army built four or five recreation halls that were in constant use for dances, basketball, movies, and, beginning on August 8, 1944, "hillbilly" shows featuring the stars of WNOX's "Mid-Day Merry Go Round."

Late in 1944, Fowler began putting a group together to back him up on personal appearances. In a reference to his own origins in the red hills of Georgia, he called the band the Georgia Clodhoppers. He began manning it with fellow north Georgia boys— *the* North Georgia Boys, in fact, a gospel trio he had known back in Rome. He first recruited Curly Kinsey to sing bass and play guitar. In January of 1945, tenor singer and standup bassist "Little" Johnny New joined. When Lon "Deacon" Freeman, the third North Georgia Boy, arrived in 1946, they would comprise the first Oak Ridge Quartet.

Fowler's background was gospel, but he had a reputation in country music as the co-writer of the Eddy Arnold hit "Mommy, Please Stay Home with Me Tonight." In 1945, at the invitation of the newly

formed Capitol Records, Fowler took his band, along
with Chet Atkins, to a studio in Atlanta, where
Wallace Fowler and His Georgia Clodhoppers cut
their first records—"Propaganda Papa" and "A
Mother's Prayer." It was Fowler's first secular record and Atkins's first recording session.

The gospel quartet within the Georgia Clodhoppers
was known as the Oak Ridge Quartet by the fall of
1945, but *exactly* when and how they came by that
name is unclear. According to Fowler's version, published in an Oak Ridge Quartet songbook in 1949,
they were originally called the Harmony Quartet, a
common, almost generic name in gospel music. Then
they began playing weekly Saturday morning concerts for school children at an Oak Ridge recreation
center.

"The children kept asking for us to come back and
told their parents about it," Fowler wrote. "Very soon
the children's parents started coming to the concerts.
We were there for so many appearances until we felt
like all the children and their parents were our
personal friends, so we decided to name our quartet
'The Oak Ridge Quartet.' "

That has been the accepted story, and it is based on
fact. The Oak Ridge Recreation and Welfare Association inaugurated the "Child Activities Program" on
Saturday, January 6, 1945. Three weeks later, as
reported in the weekly *Oak Ridge Journal*, entertainment was provided by performers from WNOX, including Wally Fowler and his "Clod Hoppers."

The paper mentioned Fowler specifically only one
other time, on July 14, but there may have been many
more, as Fowler said there were. Johnny New remembers the group playing on a regular basis, three
or four Saturdays a month. And perhaps signifi-
cantly, the Child Activities Program ended after
September 8, 1945, one week before Fowler debuted
on the Grand Ole Opry in Nashville.

It is likely the Oak Ridgers preferred the spiritual songs to the hillbilly repertoire. These people were not rural southerners, but rather scientists and engineers brought in (even the construction workers) from northern cities. Their primary interests, according to the space in the newspaper, were classical music and church. So it would not be surprising if the adults preferred familiar hymns like "How Great Thou Art" and the children preferred familiar spirituals like "Ain't Gwine Study Wah No Mo'," to the domestic comedy of "Propaganda Papa" or the maudlin sentiment of "A Mother's Prayer."

But when it came to naming the group, Fowler's motives were probably more commercial than sentimental. Jerry Collins, a "Mid-Day Merry Go Round" performer whose dance band played Oak Ridge often, believes that the group was not named after the town until shortly after the atom bomb.

"Wally wanted to cash in on Oak Ridge," Collins said. "Once that thing happened, he jumped on it. Oak Ridge meant the bomb."

Fowler himself as much as corroborated Collins's statement in a 1983 interview with John Wooley of the *Tulsa World*. He was talking about his current group, the Sounds of Nashville Band, which he had just renamed the 16th Avenue Band in response to a recent country hit. The idea, he explained, was to take advantage of current situations, as he had done with Oak Ridge and the atomic bomb.

On September 15, 1945, Wally Fowler debuted as a solo performer on radio station WSM's "Grand Ole Opry," singing a country song, "I'm Sending You Red Roses." Minnie Pearl's *Grinder's Switch Gazette*, a monthly folio-sized newsletter published by the Opry comedienne, had this to say about Fowler and his group: "The Clodhoppers are one of the most versatile bands in the country. They all write songs, play several instruments, each is a good soloist and the group includes a quartet that is second to none. When the quartet sings the old-time spirituals, the audience always calls for more."

"The quartet" was called by name in Fowler's advertisements as early as January of 1946, but it was May or June before the "Oak Ridge Quartet" began appearing on Opry programs. Also at that time, Fowler moved to a more prestigious spot on the Opry—the 9:30–10:00 show, sponsored by Prince Albert tobacco and broadcast nationwide by NBC over a 125-station network.

The promotion was deserved, for Fowler was a bona fide star in the mold of the new, smooth, twang-free country singers exemplified by Eddy Arnold. Capitol brought the whole band to California to record. And on September 14, 1946, Fowler made the cover of *Billboard* magazine.

The Oak Ridge Quartet quickly gained its own notoriety, and the gospel group cut its first records in 1947 in Nashville at Studio C (the largest of WSM's three studios) under the direction of producer Cliffie Stone.

"We cut records for twenty-four hours 'round the clock," Deacon Freeman recalls. "They recorded everything we knew."

The records were sixteen-inch, "transcription"-size 78 rpm discs. They were sent out to deejays, who would play the appropriate band when Capitol announced the record as a new release. That first Oak Ridge Quartet "album" contained twelve songs on six 78s, including "I've Got Faith," "Jericho Road," and "Just a Little Talk with Jesus."

On Friday, November 5, 1948, Wally Fowler staged what was probably the single most important event in the history of gospel entertainment—the "first" all-night singing. He had staged all-night singings at least three times before, but this one was different. It was at the Ryman Auditorium (the Opry House), and from 11:00 P.M. to midnight the whole country could tune it in on WSM's 50,000-watt signal.

The show started at 8:00 P.M. and featured some of the biggest acts in gospel music—the Blackwood Brothers, the Speer Family, the Goodmans. By the time WSM started its broadcast, the stage was completely filled by gospel stars sitting in chairs. In front of the microphone were the emcee and the host act, Wally Fowler and the Oak Ridge Quartet—Johnny New, Deacon Freeman, Curly Blaylock (who had replaced Curly Kinsey), and Neal "Junior" Matthews, Jr. (who sang and provided guitar accompaniment).

The Oak Ridge Quartet rented the building and bought the air time on that first night. They made a profit of only $97, but they set the standard format for gospel shows for years to come. Fowler staged another all-night singing at the Ryman Auditorium on December 31, 1948. Beginning in May of 1949, the show became a regular event on the first Friday of each month.

One of the features of each show was Fowler's prayer. He was forbidden by WSM from plugging his upcoming dates, but he reasoned correctly that no one would dare stop a man in the middle of a talk with God, even if he was saying, "Dear Lord, please watch over these boys as they travel down the highway, *to Atlanta,* and please watch over all the people we hope will come out to see our show *next Friday at the Atlanta city auditorium.* . . ."

Fowler's ad copy proclaimed the act "New! Different! Versatile!" And they were all those things—especially different. They were a *spiritual* quartet, which was different from a gospel quartet like the John Daniel group.

They were white boys singing black music. It was nothing new, but it excited gospel fans in 1948 as it had excited minstrel show audiences a century earlier, the same way it would excite the first rock and roll fans in the fifties.

In talking about the Oak Ridge Quartet, Glen Allred, their guitarist from 1951 to 1952, could just as easily have been talking about Elvis Presley and the Sun Records rockabillies, who were just a few years and a few miles down the road in Memphis.

"We did an awful lot of colored spirituals, really," Allred recalled. "Some of them, coloreds never did sing, but they were written like that anyway. Wally was a good singer—still is—and could really sing a spiritual and do a lot of chanting the way the coloreds used to do it."

Deacon Freeman was "famous for his chanting of the old-time Down South Rhythm Spirituals," according to a Fowler songbook. "They call it 'rap' now," Freeman explained. "You chant it off, 'most all the way through. You could read three or four verses in the Old Testament and put it together and make spirituals out of it, and that's what we did."

In the spring of 1948, WSM offered the Oak Ridge Quartet a staff job, but Fowler wanted to stay on the road. "Wally could sit up in the front seat of the car and sleep just as good as or better than he could in a bed," Freeman said. "Actually he loved the road."

Fowler turned the offer down, and in retaliation Freeman and Curly Kinsey took off for Shreveport, Louisiana, where they helped start the Louisiana Hayride. Their new act soon ran into financial trouble—actually it was their car, and it ran into a lake—so Freeman returned to Nashville just in time for the first all-night singing.

Also joining the group in time for the first all-night singing was guitarist Neal "Junior" Matthews, Jr. Though still a teenager in 1948, he was already an accomplished musician. The son of an Opry guitarist, he had played on some of Fowler's early song demos, recorded in his father's living room.

Matthews's electric guitar would have been a radical accompaniment for a gospel quartet, but it was all right for a spiritual group like the Oak Ridge Quartet. A photo from the second all-night singing shows them on the Ryman stage with two pianos, both of them unmanned.

That would soon change. With the Oak Ridge Quartet beginning to overshadow the Clodhoppers (the hillbilly contingent would not last through 1949), Fowler made a move to bridge the gap between spiritual and gospel music. He hired Boyce Hawkins, a full-fledged gospel piano player. Like Matthews, Hawkins was a young musician (twenty-one) whom Fowler had played with years earlier when both were members of the John Daniel Quartet.

Evangelism, which would drive The Oak Ridge Boys out of gospel music in the seventies, was secondary to showmanship to gospel audiences of the late forties. And the 1949 Oak Ridge Quartet, like all the Oak Ridge Quartets to come, could put on a show. They would always open with "Dese Bones a Gwinna Rise Again" and continue with the classic spirituals—"Ain't Gwine Study Wah No Mo'," "Swing Down Chariot," or "I'se in His Care." After the spirituals came the standard Stamps-Baxter material like "Peace in the Valley." Hawkins and Matthews, both excellent musicians, could impress a crowd with a piano/guitar duet. And "Little Bashful" Johnny New would make them roll with laughter when he'd sidle up to Fowler, cock his head at a crazy angle, and, gazing wide-eyed up at him, start wailing, "I'm a Bible Loving Man." Fowler could stop a show with his smooth, anthemlike rendition of the old standard "How Great Thou Art." They'd close with some good old tunes from the Baptist hymnal.

The Oak Ridge Quartet was working around 200 dates a year, and the travel began to wear on even the younger members. In 1949, the four singers left

Fowler and went, ironically, to his hometown of Rome. They renamed themselves the Stone Mountain Quartet and performed on local radio. Eight months later, Neal Matthews was drafted and the group disbanded.

Boyce Hawkins quit music to finish high school. When he left, Fowler owed him $150. Hawkins had some of Fowler's fishing gear in the trunk of his car, and he kept it in lieu of the money. It was a preview of things to come for Fowler, only the next time it happened, ten years down the road, he would lose a lot more in the trade than his fishing gear.

Wally Fowler lost the group, but he still had bookings for the Oak Ridge Quartet to fill. So he did what he had done back in Knoxville with the North Georgia Boys—he hired an entire group. The Calvary Quartet, from Statesville, North Carolina, consisted of Bob Weber, bass; Joe Allred, tenor; Pat Patterson, lead; and Bill Campbell, guitar. The Calvary Quartet played one of Fowler's all-night singings in Winston-Salem, North Carolina, on November 8, 1949. Two-and-a-half weeks later, on November 26, they were the Oak Ridge Quartet, backing up Wally Fowler on the Grand Ole Opry.

Despite the complete changeover, there was soon a familiar face in the Oak Ridge Quartet. The tenor developed throat problems and was replaced by Johnny New. New really was new. He was sober.

During his first stint with the Oak Ridge Quartet, New had developed a problem so severe, he recalled, "I was drinking twenty-four hours a day, seven days a week.... I got to where I couldn't even feed myself."

By the time the quartet moved to Rome, he had sobered up, and with the help of Alcoholics Anonymous, he felt he could handle the road again. He also felt he owed something to the audiences, so in addition to his $125-a-week salary, he asked for a spot on the show to give his testimony.

"I wanted people to know I'd changed," he said. "Most of the places where they'd seen me drunk, they got to see me sober."

In the fall of 1951, New gave his notice, but before he left, the band was in a car wreck. New came out of it with a sore neck, which a doctor put in a brace. He tried to work out his notice, but the pain became unbearable.

"My neck was hurting, my vision was blurred, and my head was just a-killing me," he said. His doctor took off the brace. "My head just flopped over like wringing a chicken's neck—limbered over—and I became very nauseous."

Brain specialists operated, and they found what New described as "a two-tablespoon blood clot" at the base of his brain. It was removed, but his troubles were not over. He had to sue Fowler to recover any insurance money (a jury awarded him $5,000), and his health continued to worsen. His was a tragic case—a singer who could not bear to listen to music because of the pain it caused. He was finally cured, not by specialists but by a couple of preachers, and he himself later became a preacher.

When New left, Joe Allred returned. Their repertoire still resembled that of the original group, but their youthfulness gave them a certain fire, both onstage and off.

"We were just, you know, a young bunch of boys that liked the girls, like young guys now like them," said Glen Allred, their guitarist from 1951 to 1952. "That Bob Weber, I guess he was probably the best-looking guy in the group. I mean, he had a different girl every night, and I mean the prettiest girl in the whole place."

Bob Weber was not the type just to stand still and look good, Allred added. "That cottonpicker would do anything to sell, to get the crowd going. He got to where he was jumping over pianos when we got to an encore—grands or uprights, whatever we had."

On October 4, 1951, the Oak Ridge Quartet played Evansville, Indiana. Mrs. Minnie Huff took the road-weary boys to her house for a home-cooked meal. She gave the sixteen-year-old guitar player Glen Allred a picture of Jesus, which he carries in his wallet to this day. On the back, she wrote, along with the date, "Oak Ridge Boys." It would be more than a decade before they would officially call themselves "Boys."

By the end of 1951, Wally Fowler was appearing with the Oak Ridge Quartet only on the big gospel shows and staying home during the week. His ambition to be the next Eddy Arnold had probably faded with the Georgia Clodhoppers, who took their final bow before the Calvary Quartet arrived. He had the smooth, personable voice, but he didn't have much charisma onstage. He soothed his ego with food (Deacon Freeman says he weighed near 300 pounds) and with the growing popularity of his all-night singings. He promoted almost 250 shows in 1951, and in late 1952 he offered Bob Weber ownership of the Oak Ridge Quartet in exchange for a $10,000 loan. Weber accepted, although he says Fowler never paid him back.

In Fowler's absences, the baritone singer would sing lead and Glen Allred would take over the baritone. Unfortunately, Allred was admittedly not much of a singer at that time. When Weber hired Bob Prather, a good singer and a songwriter as well, Allred was told he was no longer needed.

"It really hurt me," he said. "I was in a hotel room by myself and cried for I don't know how long. I thought I was a has-been at seventeen. I really enjoyed that year-and-a-half. A bunch of young boys, we really had a good time."

In 1953, Calvin Newton joined the Oak Ridge Quartet, and their show progressed from exciting to outrageous. Bob Weber was already jumping over pianos. Now they had a guy who jumped off the stage into the audience.

"The first time I did it, I liked to broke my leg," said Newton, whose speaking voice is still loaded with urgency. "I thought the stage was four feet, and it was seven. But boy, it really tore 'em up. I was a crazy kid. I thought there was nothing I couldn't do."

Newton, as the newest member, was designated as driver of one of the two Cadillac limos the group traveled in. "I thought it was an honor," he said. "I loved to drive fast."

He had to drive fast to make some of Fowler's bookings. They often played "bicycle" dates, where a four-act show would be booked in two different towns on the same night. Two would start in one town and two in the other, and they would hit the road for the second booking as soon as they got offstage. Occasionally they would play three-date "tricycles," and on one such date Newton said it would be impossible, even for him, to make it on time. Fowler offered to pay any speeding tickets he got, and that was all the license Newton needed.

Calvin Newton would have fit better into a Jack Kerouac novel than a gospel quartet. He was not just driving fast; he was living fast. He took amphetamines to the point of addiction, and he took women where he found them—usually in the back of the Cadillac.

"We were pioneering then, and we were pretty much little gods to our fans," he explained. "And we took undue advantage sometimes. We were all single. Sometimes we'd get through a concert and a little girl would be lying back there on the floorboards, wanting one of us to take her home. We generally did."

Tenor Joe Allred quit and was replaced by Cat Freeman, whose voice was so high and clear that he had been nicknamed "Sister Cat." In contrast, Newton on the lead part had a rough edge to his voice and sang with a lot of dynamic swoops.

The variety of tones and styles was the basis of the Oak Ridge Quartet's calling card, a song called "Go Out to the Program." It was barely a song, just a verse that encouraged the listener to go out to a gospel show. But in the middle, they mimicked their fellow gospel stars—the Chuck Wagon Gang, the Speer Family, the Statesmen.

Like many of the tunes in the original Oak Ridge repertoire, "Go Out to the Program" was black music. Bob Weber discovered it.

"We'd go into record stores and listen to all the black groups," Weber said. "We found this one in Dothan, Alabama." Calvin Newton arranged it to ridicule white acts, and the routine became so popular that it endured across a void when the Oak Ridge Quartet did not even exist.

By the mid-fifties, the all-night singings were gaining national attention. *Time, Collier's*, and *The Saturday Evening Post* all did stories on the phenomenon. The latter included this report from Atlanta's Municipal Auditorium: "Out front a tenor in the Oak Ridge Quartet had just struck a high note, and the mob in the auditorium had responded in a manner that recalled the days when the bobby-soxers of yesteryear discovered Frank Sinatra. Women out there shrieked, and a couple of young girls rushed to the stage edge to snap pictures of the tenor, who was holding that high note the way a trumpet player prolongs a ride."

And later in the article, the Oak Ridge Quartet was reported "livening up their performance with gyrations in the style of the Crew Cuts of 'pops' fame and comedy that bordered on slapstick."

The articles also contained impressive attendance figures that made it sound like the "sawdust trail"— the old term for the gospel road—had turned into a golden highway. Ironically, the Oak Ridge Quartet, one of the top five gospel acts, was about to go under.

Bob Weber's casual attitude toward management may have been a factor. He was only twenty-one when he took over from Fowler.

"It was a fun time, I guess you might say," he recalled. "We didn't have much 'business' to our deal. We just had a good time."

Whether it was Weber's management, the loss of group identity due to constant personnel changes, or, as Calvin Newton believes, the vindictive jealousy of some of the more well-established groups, the bottom line was clear.

"The group needed bookings and couldn't get them," Weber said.

In late 1956, with the group once again based in North Carolina, Weber left to work for the Chuck Wagon Gang, and Newton announced from the stage in Atlanta that he was leaving for a career as a nightclub singer. Before the year was out, the Oak Ridge Quartet disbanded.

Meanwhile, back in Nashville, Wally Fowler put the word out that he was forming a new backup group to be called the Country Boys. He had discovered a young singer from Pulaski, Tennessee, whose smooth, personable voice sounded remarkably like Fowler's. His name was E. Smith "Smitty" Gatlin, and, with Fowler guiding him, he would lead the new quartet.

In Decatur, Illinois, nineteen-year-old Ronnie Page heard the news and came to Nashville to try out. Page passed his audition, but there was a problem—the Country Boys weren't quite ready to roll. And there was another problem. Page's boss at the GMAC office back home had made good on his promise to fire him if he went to audition. So Fowler offered him a job as a gofer in return for room and board until the Country Boys could get going.

While he was waiting, Page met the Oak Ridge Quartet backstage at the Ryman. Their bass singer, Bob Weber, had just quit, and they needed a fill-in for two months until the man they wanted, Armand Morales (who would become a cornerstone of the Imperials quartet) got out of the Army. Page was a baritone, but a cocky baritone, and he recommended himself for the bass position.

"They paid me $50 a week, and I was making more money than any of 'em," he recalled. They were, in fact, in deep financial trouble. They didn't even last the two months.

The opportunistic Fowler had cashed in on the Oak Ridge name a decade earlier. Now, with the Weber group disbanded, he tried to cash in on the Oak Ridge *Quartet* name. At his suggestion, the Country Boys became the "new" Oak Ridge Quartet.

Smitty Gatlin had Ronnie Page to sing baritone. He recruited a tenor, Hobart Evans, and a pianist, Powell Hassell, from the Rainbow Quartet, a part-time group from Tuscaloosa, Alabama. Bill Smith, a bass singer from Valdosta, Georgia, filled out the new Oak Ridge Quartet.

Gatlin took them to Pulaski, seventy-five miles south of Nashville, where they spent the last week of 1956 working up the Oak Ridge Quartet repertoire. "At the end of that week, we were a professional quartet," Page said. "We thought we knew all the answers, and we didn't know what the questions were yet."

After a sort of preview debut at a New Year's Eve all-night singing in Birmingham, they played their first real show—shows, actually—on a "bicycle" date between Sheffield and Decatur, Alabama on January 3, 1957. Page remembered two things about the dates. One was their clothing—brown and white tweed jackets, brown pants, and white shoes. The other was having to make two trips between the

towns at breakneck speed, thanks to a Fowler mix-up
on the order of the shows.

Bill Smith, the bass singer, didn't last long.

"He had the prettiest, low-downdest voice you ever
heard in your life," Ronnie Page said, "and not a lick
of sense." He gave an example: "One night we were
singing a song called 'There's a Leak in This Old
Building.' It started out, the bass sang, 'Wellll, there's
a leak in this old building,' the title of the song. I gave
it a great big buildup and said, 'Now here's a song,
"There's a Leak in This Old Building.' " Bill steps up
to the microphone and says, 'Wellll . . .' Turns around.
'I forgot the words.' "

Smith was quickly replaced by Herman Harper,
who dropped out of Falls Business College to be a
full-time gospel singer. Harper had just turned eighteen, and the oldest group member, Powell Hassell,
was only twenty-two. They were five young bucks out
to burn up the sawdust trail.

"That first year was something else," Harper said.
"We liked to starved. Smitty decided when he organized the group that he wanted to manage and more
or less own the group, so he put us on salary. He was
paying me $75 a week. That lasted about five weeks,
and Smitty went broke."

Consequently, they went into a partnership and
everyone went broke. A photo from that period tells
the story. It shows the four singers in fancy coats with
Hassell at the piano in a black suit.

"We were so poor we couldn't buy another suit,"
Hassell said. "When Bill Smith left, nobody could
wear his clothes. So I gave Herman my outfit. We
decided, if somebody was going to be different, it's
better for the piano player to be different."

Even though the crowds were sometimes small, the
old Oak Ridge material and stage routines still
brought them to their feet. Page had learned the
show during his short stint with the old group, and he

taught the new boys one of the showstoppers, "Tearing Down the Kingdoms."

"Before the show started," he said, "one of us would very quietly put a white Bible on the edge of the stage, out towards the front. No one would really even know it was there, a book laying up on the stage. When we did that song, we did a series of choruses where we changed keys every chorus. The theme of it was 'We're looking for the rock that was hewn out of the mountain, came tearing down the kingdoms of the world. Where is the rock?'

"And then we were walking very slowly as a quartet, all four of us, toward the Bible. Then it was 'Thank God we've found the rock,' our hands all at the same time would touch the Bible. Then very slowly we rose, very slowly, during the entire chorus. And it's changing keys. It's going higher each time. And then the last chorus we're standing, and then we sang, 'We're going home with the rock.' Then we put our hands up all at the same time, 'Home with the rock.' Boy, it would tear a crowd up."

Hassell and Evans, in their Tuscaloosa group, had performed the Oak Ridge Quartet's famous "Go Out to the Program." They taught it to the new group, and once again the song became, as Page put it, "our sugar stick."

Eighteen years later, Johnny Cash would bail a struggling Oak Ridge group out of near-bankruptcy by adding them to his show. In 1957, it was Marty Robbins who helped them, temporarily at least, avoid starvation by hiring them on a series of fair dates. The pay was only $120 per show, and there were only bunks enough on the bus for Robbins's band (the quartet slept during the daytime), but at least they had no travel expenses. And they did get to sing southern quartet music where it had never been heard before, in areas of the Northeast, West, Northwest, and practically every major city across Canada.

When the fair season ended, the Oak Ridge Quartet

almost ended, too. Fowler wasn't coming through with dates, and the group, being so new to the business, didn't know any other promoters. So in late 1957, they decided to find straight jobs where they could rehearse at night and sing on weekends. Hassell quit and was replaced by Tommy Fairchild, yet another alumnus of the John Daniel Quartet. Hobart Evans, the original tenor, had already been forced to leave the group when a stove blew up in his face. His replacement also left when they decided to drop down to part-time.

The first order of business after everyone found a job was to find a tenor singer. They lowered their musical arrangements and put Gatlin on tenor and Fairchild on lead until they found Willie Wynn. They heard about Wynn at an all-night singing in Atlanta. He was home sick with the flu, so at intermission Gatlin went to Wynn's apartment.

Wynn put on an overcoat and auditioned on the second half of the show. "Little Willie" could sing, all right, but he was obviously a hayseed. Here was a guy who had named his high school group the FFA Quartet because they were all Future Farmers of America. He looked like he had just ridden in on a produce truck from his hometown of Moultrie, Georgia. He weighed 116 pounds, and his straw-colored hair was chopped down to a GI bristle.

But he could sing, and Gatlin offered him the job. He had to wait for his wife to deliver a baby before he could move to Nashville and join the group. But when he did, Harper said, "He really helped us a lot. Everybody loved him."

Wally Fowler wasn't doing much better than the Oak Ridge Quartet, and he owed them somewhere between $2,500 and $3,000 by Harper's estimate. In a deal similar to the one he had made with Bob Weber in 1952, Fowler gave Smitty Gatlin ownership of the name in return for forgiving the debt.

It didn't seem like such a bad deal at the time for

Fowler. After all, he didn't own the name to begin with, having never bought it back from Bob Weber. And in the probable event that the group folded, he could always start yet another Oak Ridge Quartet and save $3,000 in the process.

It would prove to be one of the worst business deals since the Indians traded Manhattan for a pile of wampum.

Despite their regular jobs, the Oak Ridge Quartet acted like a full-time professional group. They were good enough to attract the interest of Cadence Records, a Chicago label. They auditioned in Gatlin's living room and cut their first album at RCA's famous Studio B. They never sold enough albums to see a royalty check from Cadence, but just having an album on a known label boosted their reputation. By the middle of 1959, they were being offered more dates than they could work, so they put themselves on a small salary and returned to the road full-time.

They went through several vehicles and then bought a bus—a 1939 GMC "four-banger" (four-cylinder) that would take them down the sawdust trail at a hundred miles an hour. Now it wasn't a matter of when they would make their dates; it was *if*.

"We used to have a few wrecks—a lot," Willie Wynn explained. Some of their wrecks were tragic, like the one that made life torturous for Johnny New. Some were comic, like the time William Lee Golden rammed into the back of the Speer Family bus, causing Brock Speer to faint in Willie Wynn's arms.

Most of the wreck stories, however, have one scene in common: Willie Wynn at the wheel. If Wynn wasn't the worst driver, he was the most notorious. One gag photograph shows the bus with the front completely smashed in, the windshield broken, and poor Little Willie's lifeless form draped out the front window.

Wynn's greatest wreck came one Thanksgiving

Eve just before dawn on a highway in northern Mississippi.

"I hit a mule," he said. He didn't just hit it; he hit it at eighty miles per hour. It came through the windshield and smashed all over the front cabin of the bus.

What ended up as a funny story (except to the mule, who died) was almost a tragedy. Smitty Gatlin had been standing in the stairwell at the front of the bus, talking to Wynn before going to bed. He had just gotten to his bunk when the mule hit, shoving in the front of the bus at the very spot he had been standing.

When the quartet found jobs in 1958, Ronnie Page worked as a deejay and music director at a radio station. In 1960, he was offered a job by a Nashville television station hosting a gospel TV show. In trying to work the show around the schedules of the gospel artists, he became a pioneer in the field of music video, but he also became overloaded with work. By 1962, he had to make a choice, and he left the Oak Ridge Quartet for TV.

By now the group had some records to sell. In 1959, they recorded an album for Monument. Then they made two for Skylite, a company owned by the Statesmen and the Blackwood Brothers. In the early sixties they made two albums for Starday and one for United Artists.

In 1962, with Gary McSpadden now singing baritone, they cut the first of two albums for Warner Brothers that were not only pivotal to their careers but highly influential on other groups as well. Looking for something new and innovative, they went into the studio with a full complement of Nashville's hottest session musicians. It was still gospel music, but the lone piano accompaniment had been replaced by the "Nashville Sound," a smooth, echo-laden, rhythm-guitar-based texture that was becoming the rage among pop artists.

Their producer, Bud Praeger, suggested that the

name Oak Ridge Quartet sounded a little old-fogyish for the new "contemporary" sound, as it would come to be called. The group agreed, and the album was called *The Oak Ridge Boys with the Sounds of Nashville*. They were The Oak Ridge Boys forever after.

The Nashville Sound was not the only sound going in the early sixties. Folk music was new, fresh, and, above all, different from anything in gospel, and The Oak Ridge Boys jumped on it. Their next album for Warner Brothers bore the catchy title *Folk-Minded Spirituals for Spiritual-Minded Folks*.

Down in south Alabama, a young gospel fan named William Lee "Bill" Golden heard the two Warner Brothers albums and became hooked on The Oak Ridge Boys, rarely missing a show when they were in the area.

"They were always exciting, always entertaining," Golden recalled. "When The Oak Ridge Boys came on stage, they woke the crowd up. They could outsing any of the quartets there, outperform them. They just looked like they were having more fun than everybody else there."

"Bill Golden *loved* The Oak Ridge Boys," Harper said, but actually he only loved them up to a point— the point at which Gary McSpadden was replaced by Jim Hammill on the baritone part. McSpadden had dark wavy hair and the sharp looks of a young man who was going places. Hammill was overweight and at that time had his hair slicked down (he would later proudly wear it in a "Parris Island" crew cut). In Golden's view, Hammill was detrimental to the Oaks' high-energy, trailblazing ways.

Bill knew the Oaks—his group, the Pilots Trio, had worked some shows with them—and in the fall of 1964, he drove to Nashville to try to rectify the damage he thought Hammill had done to the group. He offered himself as baritone singer. Gatlin agreed in principle but did not act immediately. Bill went back to his paper mill job and waited.

He didn't have to wait long.

"We couldn't get along with Hammill, and we didn't keep anybody around we couldn't get along with," Herman Harper recalled. Hammill ended up with the Kingsmen quartet, where the bad blood between him and the Oaks would later come to a boil.

In the first days of 1965, Bill Golden drove the 350 miles from Brewton, Alabama, to Nashville to become the baritone singer for The Oak Ridge Boys.

Harper said he wasn't sure if Bill could sing, but he knew one thing: "He was a real good-looking guy, real sharp. He made the group look good."

As Harper soon found out, he *could* sing.

"Bill could always blend," Harper said. "He and Smitty and Willie could blend so good. I've always thought he was one of the best baritones in gospel music for blending."

And more importantly for the long run, Bill's attitude was perfect for a group that was becoming more and more controversial. Harper described him as a "deep thinker" and as someone always thinking several years ahead.

The Oak Ridge Boys were already hearing the backlash from the traditional gospel crowd for "jiving up" the music on the Warner Brothers albums. They caused even more controversy when they decided to become the first act to go on a gospel stage without neckties. They showed up in Madison, North Carolina, in gold coats and light blue turtlenecks, and the promoter was not going to let them onstage.

"We took it to the fans," Harper recalled. "We went on the stage and told them they weren't going to let us sing. They raised the roof. That was the end of that."

With The Oak Ridge Boys doing so well now, Wally Fowler decided it was time for him to get his piece of the pie. Forgetting that he no longer owned the name, he started a new Oak Ridge Quartet and began booking them on gospel shows. The real Oak Ridge Quartet—now Boys—were not amused, and on October 5, 1964, Smitty Gatlin filed suit.

Just over a year later, on October 10, 1965, David-son County (Nashville) Chancellor Alfred T. Adams decreed that Gatlin owned the name. Fowler was enjoined from using the name Oak Ridge Quartet or anything confusingly similar, and he also had to pay the $49.25 in court costs.

Also in 1965, The Oak Ridge Boys played a part in another important innovation in gospel music. They signed a booking agreement with Don Light, who had just formed the first exclusively gospel booking agency. Up until then, most acts had booked them-selves and seldom, if ever, worked with a signed contract.

With Don Light handling their booking and their record albums selling well, the future looked great for The Oak Ridge Boys.

But they almost didn't make it to that future.

In the spring of 1966, Smitty Gatlin announced he was leaving the group for a job as minister of music at the First Baptist Church in Dallas. His departure was a devastating blow since he managed the group as well as sang lead. Harper, with encouragement from Don Light, took over the management, which was no small responsibility.

"We were really progressing," he said. "There was really a lot to do."

The most difficult thing to do was to replace Smitty, one of the most respected singers in gospel music. Their first choice was Duane Allen, whom they knew as the former baritone singer with the Prophets quartet. They called him in Texas and offered him a job.

Duane had two other offers—one from the States-men and one from the Selective Service. He went to Dallas for his physical, but because of a childhood heart problem he was turned down. He came back home and tried to contact the Oaks but couldn't.

Confident that they still wanted him, or if they didn't the Statesmen or possibly the Cathedral Quartet did, Duane bought a new car and drove to Nashville. He arrived at Don Light's office (then in the RCA building) as the secretary was trying to call him in Texas. The Oak Ridge Boys were in the next room, talking about disbanding.

"If we hadn't gotten somebody of Duane's caliber, we might have," Harper said.

Duane went with them to a church they used for rehearsals. He sang two songs, "Farther Along" and "In the Shelter of His Arms," and then the group stepped off into a side room. Five minutes later Duane Allen was the lead singer and a full partner in The Oak Ridge Boys.

William Lee Golden is one of the most sincere people I know. He is very sincere, which is one of the reasons he is so well liked by our fans. He's very unselfish, one of the most giving people I know.—
Richard Sterban

*Sometimes, he is the hardest person in the world to communicate with. Other times, he is the easiest. He is a simple man, a good man. All you have to do is look in his eyes to see the honesty, the goodness he possesses.—*Joe Bonsall

*We've spent twenty-one years together. I think that speaks for itself.—*Duane Allen

3

WILLIAM LEE GOLDEN:

MOTHER NATURE'S SON

With his long, flowing hair and beard that nearly reach his waist, William Lee Golden is the most instantly recognizable member of The Oak Ridge Boys.

The soft-spoken, enigmatic baritone is a twentieth-century mountain man who pursues a lifestyle that has sparked both curiosity and criticism from the public and his musical partners, as it has brought him a cherished inner peace. It is an image that contrasts sharply with one writer's description of Golden in the late 1970s as "the Barry Gibb of country music."

But whether pursuing his vision of an unlimited career for The Oak Ridge Boys or his own vision of personal truth, William Lee has pursued his spiritual quests with uncommon courage and faith.

In typical Golden fashion, he dismisses the curiosity about and criticism of his life with a shy, warm smile and a shrug.

If you were to search for the beginnings of Golden's evolution into the back-to-the-basics man he is today, you would have to go beyond 1980, when he decided to let his hair grow and drop his nickname, Bill, in favor of William Lee. You would need to take a close look at his heritage and family environment. William Lee's lifestyle, you see, is not so much an evolution as it is a return to the roots and influences of his rural upbringing.

William Lee "Bill" Golden was born January 12, 1939, at his family's farm near Brewton, Alabama, a town of about 500 people located near the Florida state line. He is the second of three children. His sister Lanette was the oldest, his brother Ronnie the youngest.

His parents, Luke and Ruth Golden, farmed about half of their eighty acres of land with a pair of mules. Among the crops they grew were cotton, corn, and soybeans.

To say the Golden family led a rustic lifestyle would be quite accurate.

"We lived more primitively than the rest of our relatives," William Lee recalls. "There were twelve or thirteen kids in Dad's family. He was the third of triplets. We lived in the country. We did not have running water, electricity, a telephone, or a car at home. I didn't experience those things until I started school. I never knew they existed, really. I remember when Dad bought a tractor. We had it before we had the pickup and, later, the car."

William Lee was named for two of his relatives.

"The William came from my great-grandfather on my mother's side. The Lee came from my grand-father Golden."

Lee Rush Golden was a minister. One of young William Lee's fondest and earliest musical memories is of his grandfather Golden playing fiddle. One of his uncles led singers in church.

"I was attracted to music at a very young age. Before I started school, I was singing in church. My sister taught me to play guitar and sing. She also played the mandolin, and we used to sing duets. My brother sang some with us, too. We would sing at home, practice a lot."

The Golden family owned a battery-powered radio, but they didn't need a radio for the home to be filled with music.

"We sang mostly gospel songs and spirituals. We also sang a lot of Hank Williams songs, particularly 'I Saw the Light.'"

Lanette and William Lee sang on Brewton radio station WEBJ for several years, starting when he was but seven years old. They sang on their grandfather Golden's radio show.

Like any other boy reared on a farm, Golden had chores to do.

"I thought about singing a lot when I was plowing the fields," he recalls. "We grew up in the fields, and I sang a lot then. Sometimes, as the day flows on, your spirit can be taken to a different place with music. Singing was always a great feeling of freedom for me. I could sing as loud as I wanted."

When the chores were done, though, it was time to put away the tools and bring out the guitars and mandolins for a family singing.

"We would gather on the front porch and play and sing for hours. I have lots of good memories about growing up. They flood me whenever I go home."

His sister has fond memories of her own about growing up with William Lee.

"He was always shy around other people, but he was a real clown around the family. He used to entertain us after supper every night, mimicking people from around town. I think William sang with me on our Granddaddy Golden's show out of duty or because it was expected of him. It wasn't until he got into school that he really took an interest in music."

But some of William Lee's most cherished childhood moments came when he would go out into the
woods for several days at a time and feel the elo-
quence of silence. It was in these moments that the
young William Lee began to get in touch with himself, with the sounds, scents, and nuances of nature.

"I lost touch with that after I left home," he says.

Singing and music were uppermost in his interests.
While country and gospel were his earliest influences, it didn't take long for the family's battery-
powered radio to open a new world to him.

"We heard all of the early rock and roll. Elvis
Presley, Carl Perkins, Little Richard, Jerry Lee
Lewis, Chuck Berry. I loved it. I loved all of it."

He loved it so much that when a talent contest was
held in his high school William Lee played guitar and
sang Elvis Presley's "Hound Dog" as his entry. Also,
while in high school, he began singing with his own
group at special events and at churches in Brewton.

The pursuit of academics, however, didn't always
agree with the young Golden.

"I would walk out in the middle of class if I got
bored. I couldn't have fun there. Rather than disturb
people, I got up and left. The principal and I had
arguments about my schooling. He thought I was a
bad kid. I just had too much fun. I just usually made
passing grades, sometimes failing ones. I had to go to
summer school to graduate from high school."

His aspirations had little to do with what was going
on in the classroom.

"Singing baritone harmony for more than twenty
years may not have been what most of the people who
went to high school at home dreamed about doing.
But it was my dream."

While he was still a high school student, an all-
night gospel singing was held in Brewton featuring
several southern gospel quartets. One of them was
the Oak Ridge Quartet.

"They were real entertainers. During part of their program they would imitate four or five of the top gospel groups. They would mimic them and sing their songs just about like them. They showed a lot of talent and were versatile. They were wholesome, family entertainment."

In 1957, during his senior year, he married his junior high school sweetheart, Frogene. They would become the parents of three sons, Rusty (William Lee II), Craig, and Christopher. Rusty was born January 3, 1959; Craig on October 20, 1960, and Christopher on October 17, 1962.

After summer school and graduation in 1958, he went to work for a paper mill in Brewton. He spent nearly five years there and sang part-time with a group in Florida.

In the late 1950s and early 1960s, the Oaks had become serious recording artists. Gary McSpadden, now a member of the Bill Gaither Trio and the New Gaither Vocal Band, was the baritone singer.

With McSpadden, the Oak Ridge Quartet became The Oak Ridge Boys and recorded two albums for Warner Brothers that would prove to be a prime influence on Golden—*The Oak Ridge Boys with the Sounds of Nashville* and *Folk-Minded Spirituals for Spiritual-Minded Folks.*

"This was the group that turned me on to The Oak Ridge Boys," William Lee says. "It was about the same time the Beatles started hitting in Europe. The Oaks really stimulated me. They were really taking a modern musical approach. Becoming an Oak Ridge Boy was the most important thing in the world to me."

Whenever the Oaks came to the area, William Lee was there. Occasionally his group, the Pilots Trio, performed at some concerts with the Oaks.

"I got to know some of the guys casually, especially Smitty Gatlin. I kept in touch with him. I felt like sharing my ideas about music, singing, harmonies, and things. So, I asked him about singing baritone. I told him if there was an opening, I'd like to try out."

Golden was hopeful it would work out. McSpadden had left the group and was replaced by Jim Hammill, whose appearance and approach to singing was radically different from that of the youthful, energetic McSpadden.

When Hammill joined, Golden said, "I thought the group lost the appeal, the charisma, the enthusiasm. I personally didn't think that Jim Hammill and his approach to singing—to him it's a ministry; to me it was clean, fun entertainment—I didn't think he fit The Oak Ridge Boys."

In the fall of 1964, Golden drove to Nashville to discuss the baritone spot with Gatlin and his vision for the Oaks. While Gatlin didn't offer the job to Golden at that time, he did arrange an audition for him with the Speers.

"I couldn't read music, so the Speers turned me down," he said.

So Golden went back to Brewton. In January 1965, he got the call he'd been waiting for. The baritone spot in The Oak Ridge Boys was his.

"They told me they were in the market for a baritone, if I was interested. I said, 'Sure.' Smitty kidded me later that he had told the guys that I might not sing too good, but I was willing to learn."

So, Golden packed up the family and headed for Nashville.

"My dad would rather we had not left Alabama," he says. "He didn't like the idea of the family being separated. But there was a need in my life to make music, a need I've felt since I was a young boy. I knew what it involved and that I would have to leave home."

William Lee knew he had to seek what he felt he was meant to do.

"I saw my first snowfall on that trip to Nashville,"

William Lee recalls. "I had grown up in southern Alabama and had never seen snow. On that trip, I got to see a blizzard."

In those early days, a vision for the future was beginning to form in William Lee's mind.

"I felt The Oak Ridge Boys were leaders in harmony and in updating music. I felt we could continue to be leaders, set some trends. I felt we could expand gospel music and broaden its horizons."

The wheels already were turning. The Golden quality that Herman Harper would call "deep thinking years ahead" had begun.

Duane Allen, who would join the Oaks a year after Golden, phrased it another way.

"William Lee is always out there thinking and dreaming. He has always been a dreamer and an innovator. He used to think in concepts that we couldn't even dream of, and they have become reality."

It was Golden who had the vision of an Oak Ridge Boys that could conquer any musical realm, stretch the limits of gospel music, and shatter stereotypes of a group's image.

"I knew that The Oak Ridge Boys did not have mass acceptance for years because there were all these people that had all these stereotyped opinions about the group. And that always bothered me because I thought that the Oaks represented some feeling that was exciting. It still does."

One of the first stereotypes Golden shattered was the traditional image of a gospel group. It was at his insistence that the Oaks changed their wardrobes from matching suits and ties to snappy Edwardian suits and white turtlenecks. More than one church congregation was horrified with the Oaks' flaunting of tradition.

Along with the wardrobe changes came longer hair. In the late 1960s, rock and roll musicians were wearing hair as long as William Lee's is today. But, in gospel music, it was considered long if it grew over the collar.

If all that weren't enough, the Oaks were also working with an energetic rock-style band. That made the Oaks a controversial act in the 1970s and made them the target of sniping by other gospel artists.

As one of the promoters of the International Gospel Song Festival in Nashville in 1970, William Lee brought together all kinds of gospel acts for a two-day show. It was during that show that the Oaks brought out a rock and roll drummer. That drummer, Mark Ellerbee, would exert an enormous influence on the Oaks' music.

"We could really get the crowds stirred up, and some of the acts that had to follow us weren't too pleased. They got back at us by putting us down for our hair, our high-fashion look, or the rock beat. Well, it don't take too much of that before that will ruffle your feathers a little. A few of those instances made the hair stand up on the back of my neck like a dog. Brought the fighting side out of me quick."

The "fighting side" of William Lee would be brought out quite a few times over the next few years as more conservative—and, to a degree, jealous— groups took potshots at the Oaks with regularity.

"If you're around these people all the time in gospel that are telling you how wrong you are, then sometimes you've really got to feel like you're right in order to keep going forward. Sometimes, you consider the source. Certain people, if they put you down, to me that's just more reasons why we should be doing something."

While controversy swirled around the Oaks, William Lee's personal life also was in turmoil. After fifteen years of marriage, the strain of his lifestyle on the road led him and Frogene to a divorce.

"I'm not sure if my divorce was a casualty of my

career. I don't necessarily think it was that. Marriage was not a thing I had to do. It takes two to get married, two to get divorced.

"Frogene was and is a good mother to our children. She has remarried and lives in the Nashville area. She's happy, and I'm happy. I didn't date anyone in particular for four or five years after we split." He would not remarry until 1984.

William Lee had other problems on his mind. Money. He didn't have any. As a partner with Duane Allen in the Oaks, his salary was $250 a week. His alimony and child support was $200 a week. He didn't have a place to live—just the Oaks' office. In 1976, Duane and William Lee took a $50 per week pay cut to give band members a raise. So his net income was zero.

While Golden was getting his personal life back in order, Duane Allen took over some of the management duties, primarily booking, from him.

Being broke, however, did not mean William Lee would give up his dreams. They were the key to better days ahead.

"I was constantly thinking about the music and The Oak Ridge Boys. Maybe I wanted the group to be more than what they wanted to be. I tried to push the group, the guys beyond their ambitions. I never lost sight of my goals and my visions."

Gospel concert bookings from major promoters had dwindled to a handful in 1975 and 1976, and William Lee knew it was time to get out of gospel music. Some acts were campaigning to keep promoters from booking the Oaks, attacks from the stage by other acts intensified, and work was drying up.

"I realized we had no future there."

William Lee felt the group's moving from Heartwarming, a gospal label, to Columbia in 1973 would help broaden the group's appeal. But that had not worked either.

"We went from being the top act at Heartwarming

to the bottom of Columbia, especially in terms of priorities. We got caught in a political thing, a change of regime. We were lost in the shuffle."

As times got worse, William Lee kept a positive attitude.

"Sometimes you have to go under to climb up. It's kind of like a seed—you have to go underground to sprout roots. We were broke, but we were trying to be honest in our way of gospel. We didn't pretend to be anything but what we were . . . we were entertainers."

The Oaks got released from Columbia in 1976 and were signed to ABC-Dot Records (now MCA), a move engineered by their booking agent and new manager, Jim Halsey.

"We knew he was capable of doing all that," William Lee says. "He worked us in Las Vegas for two years and kept us surviving. Before that, so did Johnny Cash."

When success rolled in in the form of "Ya'll Come Back Saloon" and other hits, William Lee was pleased, yet not particularly surprised.

"It was a thrill, a challenge, excitement. Not everyone can relate to it, where music might take us on our journey. There were things we had to go through, experience, then rededicate ourselves to the music.

"Every day has its own memories. Seems as we continue to grow and change, the concept sometimes changes. A lot of times I see I've made a lot of mistakes, probably more than anyone. I still do make them, sometimes—a lot of times—out of ignorance, rather than intentional."

But in May 1979, William Lee showed another sample of his visionary thinking when he told *People* magazine, "Inevitably, our music will cross all borders."

That crossing was achieved by "Elvira," a song that reached #1 on the country and pop charts, earning the Oaks a rare platinum single for sales of more than two million copies.

"To me, 'Elvira' finally put The Oak Ridge Boys into the league of entertainment that I knew the group was capable of achieving. And I thought we should have been in that league before that, but maybe we mentally were not ready to accept that responsibility of playing and singing in the mainstream of the entertainment marketplace."

"Elvira" signaled another change in The Oak Ridge Boys—William Lee began his personal quest for fulfillment. The first outward sign came when, on Christmas of 1979, he decided to quit cutting his hair. The following Thanksgiving, he quit trimming his beard.

The inner signs of a need for change came earlier.

"I felt very incomplete. Through the growth of life and my maturing as a man, I realized I didn't know a lot of things. I went to the wilderness to seek my own visions. I find a lot more peace and understanding with myself and people around me because of that. I have to be honest with who I am and what I am. I come from the ancient teachings of the primitive ways of life . . . of peace and harmony with all those around us—two-legged, four-legged, winged creatures. I grew up with that atmosphere. I knew what preparing the wood for fire, getting kindling, keeping the fire, the changing of the seasons—what it all meant. It was another year of life. That was the first thing of life I remember. The trees, the changing of seasons. I've gone back to my roots."

To some people, the interest in the American primitive may seem more like an eccentricity. But it is the way William Lee stays in touch with himself.

"I wanted to know what was real. I realized it was time to be myself, it was time to stop listening to what other people have to say about how I should live," he told Oaks publicist Kathy Gangwisch.

The turning point came when he was invited to spend a weekend in the wilderness with a group of people whose hobby was to stay in tents and hunt with bow and arrows or muzzle-loading rifles as they re-created the lifestyle of the American Indians and mountain men.

The experience was a revelation. William Lee made contact with himself, rediscovered the touch-stone that had been so meaningful to him as a youth.

"I felt like a kid again. I felt free."

He joined the American Mountain Man Association and sought out the friendship of people such as Charlie Two Feathers, a former construction supervisor who now spends his time living in the woods and selling tepee poles for a living.

As his hair started to grow, his wardrobe also underwent a drastic change. The man once described as "a snappy dresser," who had spurred the Oaks to change their fashion image, had forsaken high fashion for buckskins and American Indian clothing. His appearance was a striking turnabout from his well-groomed, sharply dressed partners.

The changes and lifestyle brought resistance and concern from Richard Sterban, Duane Allen, and Joe Bonsall.

Richard said he was very concerned about the impact Golden's changes would have on the group's fans.

"At first, I didn't understand it," Richard says. "It was drastic. I thought it was too drastic for our fans to accept. I thought it would harm us. But I observed him and how people reacted. I realized I was wrong. It was a good thing. Now I think it is a big plus for us. I realized I was wrong, and I apologized to him. He was trying to be himself."

William Lee says he wasn't worried about the fans' reaction.

"I had been going to rock and roll shows since the beginning of rock. I knew that the pop acceptance—

that audience is in for honesty and truth most of the time. I knew that the pop people that 'Elvira' brought out would not be offended by any way that I looked or dressed.

"That's when I realized that I knew that I was right and I had been right for a while. It just took a while for the music to make that place for us.

"Sometimes, there are problems getting along with our traveling brothers. But time and discussion healed it, and music is the greatest healer of all."

By the time a 1983 *People* magazine article took the "Golden problem" public, group differences had already been aired. The article, which appeared several months after the fact, was embarrassing but not destructive.

It would not, however, be the last time William Lee would cause an upheaval and concern that he was promoting himself as an entity apart from The Oak Ridge Boys. That would come later, when he started a solo album.

When the Oaks recorded their 1982 Christmas album, it gave William Lee a song many regard as his signature tune, "Thank God for Kids."

The song's success was a surprise, William Lee told reporter Kelly Delaney in *Billboard*.

"It was the type of song you didn't know about. The first time we performed it in concert was in Pine Bluff, Arkansas, when we were taping our Home Box Office cable television special. It was such a strong song that you thought at the end there might be no reaction at all. Just complete silence. I've seen that happen before. But with this song, there was a moment of silence—and then it erupted into a tremendous ovation."

The song has become a standard of sorts, especially since Golden started closing it with ". . . and grandkids, too," as a special tribute to his own grandchildren.

While William Lee revered his grandchildren and

his children, it had been nearly a decade since his divorce was final, and Golden told writer Robert K. Oermann in a *Country Rhythms* interview in April 1983 that he wasn't anxious to take another wife.

"I think marriage might be good in the right situation. And if it's not right, it sure could be a hassle to be married. I don't have anything against marriage; it's just that, ah, I guess I've never lost my passion for music. I'm not sure I could be a real good husband or not."

Apparently, he discovered he had passions for more than just music. He met model Luetta Callaway, then twenty-two, later that year.

"We had friends who had been trying to get us together for about a year. Finally, we did meet and got to know each other. We spent a few days together, then I thought about her for a while. A month later, I called her and invited her to Tennessee. We spent about nine months getting to know each other."

When Luetta's parents invited William Lee to go on a European holiday with them, he was initially undecided, then accepted. He and Luetta stayed on a few days after her parents left. Then, one night over a candlelight dinner, William Lee proposed.

The Goldens were married November 10, 1984, at Trinity Temple in Las Vegas, the bride's hometown.

Though he is twenty-two years older than his wife, the age difference doesn't seem to worry Golden.

"We're old and young enough to enjoy each other's company. Family is a very important thing to me. We are the product of the family circle. It is important to honor it, to represent our family spirit."

The touchstone for William Lee's life today is Golden Era Plantation, an historic 200-year-old, fifteen-room mansion located in Sumner County near Hendersonville, Tennessee.

William Lee bought Golden Era on July 18, 1980. July 18 also is his father's birthday.

"I moved in without any furniture," he said. "The first thing I bought was a bed. I bought antiques for the house that I felt would fit it. I didn't want to buy a bunch of furniture all at once. It just didn't seem to be the right thing to do."

There are two twenty-three-foot-tall tepees at the plantation. Sometimes, William Lee spends the night in one of them. There also is a replica of a traditional kiva behind the house. In Pueblo Indian dwellings, the kiva was a large underground ceremonial chamber used for religious purposes.

"It is a good place to think. There is a lot of power there," he says.

Nearby is a framework of tree branches for a traditional Indian sweatlodge, where William Lee occasionally hosts ceremonies of ritual purification. In the side yard there is a satellite dish.

A restored slave cabin near the main house is where William Lee often spends time because "it is real peaceful" there.

The plantation is the home for William Lee, his wife Luetta, and his sons Rusty and Chris. In addition, there are seven or eight dogs that were abandoned by previous owners and a cat named Harrah, named for the hotel and casino chain Harrah's.

"Golden Era is very much a family affair. It is a place for family expression. It is a place we can come together and be together. It is big enough that we can be as loud as we want."

Golden Era also provides Rusty and Chris a place to rehearse. Rusty is a respected Nashville songwriter and Chris is a recording artist and songwriter. William Lee is very supportive of his sons' musical careers and that of his middle son, Craig, who is a contractor and also is into video. Craig and his wife are the parents of William Lee's grandchildren.

"I used to read books about people like Davy

Crockett and the early settlers. But the mountains were a long way from where I grew up. When I acquired this place in 1980, I started getting into the history of it.

"This plantation goes back to 1780, when this part of Tennessee was still part of North Carolina. I talked to some historians and state archaeologists, and I've learned about this land's history, even before the white man moved here. There were three different Indian villages, which is about 7,000 years of cultural evolution, on this property."

According to a local historian's research, the Arcade Indians, a prehistoric tribe, once occupied this area. Others who had villages in the region were the Woodland tribe and the Mississippian Indians.

To drive the point home, William Lee retrieves arrowheads from an antique hutch. The arrowheads were found on the grounds. The house is decorated with Indian artifacts, some of which were found on the property.

"I feel a real kinship with all of this," he says.

William Lee also feels a real kinship with his own cultural history as expressed in his own musical vision. He had started some solo recording as early as his first Harvest Jam in Brewton in 1981. After the outdoor concert, he went to Muscle Shoals to record the Beatles' "Long and Winding Road"—alone.

"In the early eighties, I began to think more seriously about a solo album of songs that mean something to me. After twenty-one years, I've proven myself as a team member with The Oak Ridge Boys," Golden told publicist Kathy Gangwisch. "I always wanted to push the other guys forward. It wasn't William Lee Golden; it was The Oak Ridge Boys who had to make it. I knew I'd allowed The Oak Ridge Boys the freedom to try everything they had wanted. Now I needed that freedom.

"My intent was to satisfy myself, to fulfill myself. It

goes back to when I left Brewton. My parents didn't want me to leave. I told them I'd come back when I'd made *my* record."

But Golden's difficulty in communicating his feelings again caused some confusion and frustration that led to "a little spat," according to Joe Bonsall.

"After a while, we finally realized where Golden's heart is, what he wants to do and accomplish. Great. I can identify with that," Joe said.

American Vagabond was released in June 1986, about two months after the Oaks' album *Seasons* hit the streets. The first single was "Love Is the Only Way Out."

"It's my heart," William Lee says of the album. "It's all I have to give."

Oaks' publicist Kathy Gangwisch agrees.

"The ten songs are significant to William Lee," she said. "The lyrics reflect his feelings, his longings, his beliefs, his ideals."

Recording the solo album doesn't mean his experience with The Oak Ridge Boys has not fulfilled him, Golden says.

"It has been very rewarding on all levels. If it had not been, I would have left. More than a dollar reward, I wanted acceptance by my peers, family, and myself. Now that I've done it, I feel more spiritually satisfied. That's more important than dollars."

Despite the occasional "spats," William Lee knows how he wants the Oak Ridge Boys to be remembered.

"I want people to remember us for projecting harmony, so people can achieve goals, ambitions. I think the Oaks have been able to allow that for each of us, to grow to his fullest potential.

"We are doing what we love to do. When I did other things, music and singing moved me, moved my spirit, helping direct and stimulate certain emotions. We've seen our aspirations achieved beyond our wildest imagination. But yet, being an Oak Ridge Boy, we should always be aware of who we are, how far we've come, how much we have to be thankful for. Through music, we find expressions that, if we had tried other ways of living, we might not have found."

For William Lee Golden, always being aware of who he is means staying in touch with nature.

"There is a message there, if we are sensitive enough to listen. We find wisdom in nature because there is a lot of truth in nature. We have to stand on the solid ground, know who we are, our purpose, and our motives. We build toward the future every day."

The original Oak Ridge Quartet, circa 1946–49: (left to right) Curley Kinsey, Johnny New, Wally Fowler, and Lon "Deacon" Freeman.

Wally Fowler and the Georgia Clodhoppers, 1946: (left to right) Zeke Turner, Red Bennett, Joe Carrol, (Grand Ole Opry announcer) Grant Turner, Wally Fowler, "Deacon" Freeman, and Johnny New.

Circa 1953: (top to bottom) Joe Allred, Carlos Cook, Calvin Newton, Bob Weber, and Bobby Whitfield.

Late '50s: (left to right) Smitty Gatlin, Willie Wynn, Ron Page, and Herman Harper.

The Oak Ridge Boys (late '60s): (left to right) Noel Fox, Willie Wynn, "Bill" Golden, Tommy Fairchild, and Duane Allen.

Photo by Jimmy Moore

ORB with their 1969 Dove Awards: (left to right) Noel Fox, Tommy Fairchild, Duane Allen (front), Greg Gordon (guitarist, back), "Bill" Golden (front right), and Willie Wynn.

Courtesy of Joe Bonsall

The Keystones in the early 1970s, after Richard Sterban had left, but before Joe Bonsall (back right) and Garland Craft (front left) joined the ORB team.

Three generations of ORB bass singers, 1985: (left to right) Herman Harper, Richard Sterban, and Noel Fox.

One of the Oaks' more infamous bus wrecks, circa 1960s.

An appearance on the Grand Ole Opry in the early '70s.

The 1976 tour of the Soviet Union.

Brussells Millenium at the Grand Palace, Belgium, July
13, 1979.

Clowning on the Thames River Bridge, London, circa 1978.

In front of #10 Downing Street, home of the Prime Minister, London, circa 1978.

Photo by Norman Seeff

Publicity shot for their *Room Service* album.

Onstage at Freeport, the Grand Bahamas, March 4, 1980, with (left to right) Mel Tillis, Roy Clark, Julie Anthony, Barbi Benton, and Charly McCalin.

The Oaks on "The Tonight Show," circa late '70s.

Duane Allen is a real stabilizing factor in The Oak Ridge Boys. He is a real student of our business and of life in general. He possesses one of the most consistently good voices you'll hear anywhere. He can wake up in the morning and sing a note right on pitch.—Richard Sterban

I don't sugarcoat my opinions. I wouldn't hurt anyone's feelings on purpose, but I try to speak truthfully. I could use more tact and patience. I don't need to qualify my relationship with a friend. You qualify things when you're afraid you don't know someone well enough that they'll accept the truth.—Duane Allen

4
DUANE ALLEN:
SOLID AS A ROCK

There's a saying that "the more things change, the more they remain the same."

Duane Allen has certainly been through a lot of changes in his life and his career. But in many ways he remains the same Duane Allen who grew up on a 160-acre farm near Taylortown, Texas.

Today, Duane resolutely clings to the same two things that always have mattered the most in his life—his family and his music.

Duane David Allen was born April 29, 1943, at Taylortown, a town of "about forty or fifty people." He is the youngest of six children born to Fred and Loretta Allen. The family's farm, where his parents still live, is located about a mile from the Taylortown city limits.

"We had a very Democratic, very southern, very Baptist, very loving, very Christian home," Allen recalls. "I really don't have any wild stories from my youth. I didn't get in a whole lot of trouble—just enough in high school so they would know I was there. I feel my life at home was relatively normal with the exception of two things: I loved to sing, and I loved to play basketball."

The family raised cotton, corn, cattle, pigs, horses, goats, chickens, and peacocks. Today, Duane has kept in touch with the earth on his own acreage near his home in Hendersonville, Tennessee.

Like any member of a farm family, young Duane had chores to do.

"By the time I was old enough to work on the farm, all the jobs were pretty clear. I was the youngest, so I helped milk the cows. I usually had to stay out of school for six to eight weeks in the fall to help harvest cotton. That was usual for our part of the country, though. It was accepted with working families."

The Allen family is a very musical one.

"With the six of us kids, plus Mom and Dad, we had a double quartet in the family. At Christmastime, we all get together and sing. All my brothers and sisters can sing any of the parts. We have a ball. With our spouses, it turns into quite a session. It's wonderful."

While Duane is arguably the most successful in the music business, his two sisters also have pursued music. His older sister, Nelda, teaches music in Austin, while Martha sings in a church group.

Duane's brothers, while still active in the family's double quartets, chose other career paths. John, the oldest, served in the Texas House of Representatives for twenty years. Bob has retired from his job as a salesman with a feed company. And Fred serves as a missionary in Zambia.

"I value the way I was brought up very highly," Duane says. "It helped me to learn true values early in life—love, caring, being concerned about others, taking care of young people and older people. You do it with love with no expectation of reward. Then you get a real reward. It's instant and it's inside you. Your life is enriched so much."

Duane's parents, who have been married for more than sixty years, are proud of all of their children. But when Duane started singing at the same time he started to talk, they knew he would be something special.

"I remember my first singing experience apart from home vividly," Duane recalled. "It was at a singing school that was held at our neighborhood school. Robert S. Arnold, a gospel music writer, taught singing school in the summer. I directed my first song at that school when I was four years old. It was a big first for me. The song was 'Hand in Hand with Jesus.' "

Duane also started playing piano at age four, and by seven he was singing on the radio. A year later, he and his brothers formed a gospel quartet.

He also remembers the event that set his career dreams in motion.

"I was nine years old, and my folks took me to a concert by the Blackwood Brothers and the Statesmen in Tyler. I knew then I wanted to be in a group."

As he neared adolescence, Duane kept making musical strides. At twelve, he was directing a church choir. He was barely a teenager when he formed yet another gospel quartet with three other teens in the Taylortown area.

"In high school, I wanted to be in a gospel quartet more than anything. I remember listening to the quartets on the radio. I liked all kinds of music, but we grew up singing mainly gospel."

Duane was fifteen years old when he got his first chance to sing professionally. He had attended the Stamps Quartet Singing School in Dallas. There he was discovered by J. Howard Rogers, founder of the Paris, Texas-based Southernaires. Rogers invited Duane to join the group, and he accepted. Duane sang with the group for five years.

In addition to singing, Duane also loved basketball and played on his high school's team. Like Taylortown itself, Duane's high school was a small one.

"There were ten in my senior class. We went to our senior trip in two cars," he says, laughing. "That's the truth. Two cars." He was valedictorian of his graduating class.

When it came time to go to college, Duane had a choice—a basketball or a music scholarship.

"I decided to go with the music scholarship because, although I love both, I loved music more. And, to be honest, I wasn't tall enough to be competitive in basketball. I would have had to be a genius at basketball to make it."

So, with his future course set in his own mind, Duane enrolled at Paris Junior College in 1980, then moved on to East Texas State University to study music.

"The only real rebellion in my life came in college toward professors who put down any other kind of music other than their own. The music I had sung all my life—gospel and country—was being put down by them. I was smart enough to know they weren't that smart."

Duane's determination to stick to his goals overcame the resistance from those professors who were leading him to classical music.

"I trained with two Metropolitan Opera stars. I had the opportunity to go into that. However, I felt those people—great as they are—the best they could do is an arrangement or interpretation of something that's already written. I wanted to be part of something I could contribute to, to make a better form of music. I wanted to make a whole field of music better for my contributions. That's why I wanted to go into gospel."

Duane's calling, it seems, would be the Grand Ole Opry, not grand opera.

"There was one professor, Dr. Richardson, who stayed true all the way. He supported me. He was the only one I told what I wanted to accomplish."

The first several semesters he was in college, Duane didn't take any more music classes than he had to.

"They finally decided I should play tuba in the band. I got out in the first football game, and I didn't know which way to turn. I couldn't play the tuba and march, too."

While in college, Duane also worked part-time for three years as a disc jockey at KPLT radio in Paris. Duane was the host of a daily one-hour gospel music show.

"My show was on one hour every day. I sold my own advertising and collected the bills. I would service my advertising accounts on Saturday morning, write all the scripts that afternoon, and stay up all that night recording all seven shows."

While he was pursuing his college degree, Duane also sang in quartets, including the Taylortown Quartet and the Southernaires. He also was aware of another gospel quartet—The Oak Ridge Boys.

"I first talked with Smitty Gatlin while I was in college," Duane recalls. "It was in October of 1964. It was a pretty intense grilling. I didn't know there was going to be a change in the Oaks. He later told me that our conversation had actually been an interview. They really were feeling me out about the job. I was about a semester away from graduating from college. They didn't offer me the job, though."

The opening in the group went to William Lee. Duane will never forget the first time he saw the Oaks with Golden. It was in January 1965, the same month he graduated from college.

"I was still working at the radio station. I chartered a bus and sold seats to go see them. I was blown away when I saw them. I think it was the first concert Golden sang with them. He had long, slicked-back black hair and was wearing a blue suit. They were high-energy and exciting to watch."

After graduation, Duane went to work full-time for KPLT radio. He stayed there until April, when he was invited to become the baritone singer of the Prophets, a quartet based in Knoxville, Tennessee.

His mother and father admit they didn't like the idea of Duane's leaving home at first but realized it was his dream.

"We were very proud of him," Mrs. Allen said. "This is what he wanted to do."

Duane was there nearly a year.

"The Oaks saw me during that time and saw me perform. Herman Harper came around and talked to me a lot. Herman really liked me, and I really liked him. I always thought he was one of the finest gentlemen I ever met. He's still a good friend of mine, and my wife sings in a group with him today."

A conversation in Huntington, West Virginia, still is fresh in Duane's mind.

"He asked me some unusual questions, but I had no idea he was asking me in reference to the possibility of singing with The Oak Ridge Boys. I couldn't foresee anyone leaving."

But before the possibility could be discussed, Uncle Sam revealed he had other plans. Duane Allen was drafted.

"I rode the bus to Dallas and was at the induction center. The guys I was riding with were heading to Fort Polk, then on to Vietnam. They told me they couldn't take me because of a heart condition that I developed when I was three years old. That had been caused by being scared by some kids who were pretending to be ghosts. It accelerated my heart rate, making it beat too fast."

Duane was out of the Army and out of a job.

"The singer I had replaced in the Prophets came back with the group, and the job wasn't available anymore. The week before I left the Prophets, I came home and I had three telephone calls. One was from

the Selective Service, one from the Statesmen
Quartet, the other from The Oak Ridge Boys.

"I knew I couldn't do anything about the Selective
Service. I called the Statesmen, but they were out of
town. I called the Oaks, which was the one call I
hoped would be fruitful. They were in Nassau. There
was no way I could reach them, and they didn't know
where I was. They had been trying to reach me for a
week. They had gotten the message that I had been
drafted and was going into the Army. They didn't
know I had been rejected."

Duane was also trying to figure out who was
leaving.

"I thought it might be Golden, because Smitty and
I had talked about my singing baritone with the
group."

Since Duane couldn't reach the Oaks by telephone,
he decided he'd try to see them in person in Nashville.

"I went to the nearest automobile dealership in
Dallas and bought a brand-new 1966 Buick Riviera.
It was white, and it was loaded. I had already sold my
other car because I thought I was going in the Army.
After I got the car, I drove to Paris and loaded up the
things I had left to be sold. I went home, said good-
bye to Mama and Daddy, and headed for Nashville."

If things didn't work out, Duane had another hope.
He knew of an opening in the Cathedral Quartet.

"The Cathedrals didn't call me or offer me the job,
but I am good friends with two members of the
group. I had full intentions of giving them a call if it
didn't work out with the Oaks. I might have had a
chance with the Statesmen, too."

Duane arrived in Nashville and went to the Don
Light Talent office. Light was the manager and
booking agent for the Oaks at the time.

"I walked in the front door, and Pat Tallent, who
was the secretary, was sitting at her desk with the
telephone in her hand. Her mouth flew open, and she

couldn't speak. I told her who I was. She said, 'I know. We've been trying to get you for a week, and I'm trying to call you right now. The Oaks just told me to try you one more time, because if they can't get you this time they're going to disband the group.' Pat took me into the office, and there were the Oaks and Don Light."

"Pat told them, 'Well, you asked me to get you Duane Allen. Here he is.' They couldn't believe it. They were speechless."

Duane found out it wasn't William Lee who was leaving. It was lead singer Smitty Gatlin.

"All of a sudden they started laughing, got up, shook my hand, and hugged me. Someone said, 'Let's go somewhere and sing.' We went to the Park Avenue Baptist Church, where Herman Harper was a deacon. We sang two songs, and then the guys had me wait while they had a meeting. They came out and offered to make me a full member of the Oaks. I bought in for $1,500, plus another $100 for one-sixth of Silverline Music Company."

The thought of replacing Smitty Gatlin was scary for Duane.

"He was one of the greatest singers that was ever in our business. There was no way I could even pretend to fill his shoes. The best I could hope for was to try to make a pair of my own."

Duane will never forget his first concert with the Oaks.

"We were in Cincinnati, and there were a lot of dyed-in-the-wool Oaks fans there. One of them came up to me after we finished. She told me I was OK but that I'd never be as good as Smitty Gatlin. All of the group loved her and her family, and she loved all of them—except me. That was pretty hard to take. That happened for a while, but eventually I began to develop some people who liked me."

Duane soon realized there were only four songs in

the publishing company, two of which had been recorded. So, he started writing songs and looking for writers.

"I still had the radio bug, so I started working with WENO radio in Nashville. I did a thirty-minute show that I syndicated to about fifty or sixty stations. It was called 'Sounds of Nashville with The Oak Ridge Boys.' "

Slowly, Duane got Silverline's cash flow built up by procuring gospel rights to country songs such as "Why Me Lord," which gave him time to build up a stable of writers.

Among the gospel songs Duane has written are "He Did It All for Me," "Here's a Song for the Man," and "How Much Further Can We Go."

In 1967, Duane's life would be changed again. He met Norah Lee Stuart through The Oak Ridge Boys concerts that she and her family always attended. The family group (the Stuart Sisters Trio) were not only fans but also friends of the Oaks.

"That is how I met Norah Lee," Duane says. "When I met her, I thought, There's the blonde girl who can sing and play piano that I've always dreamed about. I broke an engagement with another woman to date Norah Lee."

Duane and Norah Lee dated about a year-and-a-half before they were married in September 1969. They are the parents of two children—a daughter, Jamie, and a son, Dee.

"Norah Lee sings with the Carol Lee Singers. They sing backup vocals at the Grand Ole Opry, as many as eight shows a week during the summer. She also does recording sessions. She's a very good singer."

Duane feels he is very fortunate to have married Norah Lee.

"We have been very lucky. We have a good marriage. Our marriage has not been in competition with, but is parallel to, our careers. It used to be

awfully rough, trying to work and keep us together.
I've tried to keep show business and family the same.
They coexist. We've worked hard at it.

"Norah Lee is the only woman I've ever wanted to
spend my life with. We were married ten years before
we had a fuss, and that one happened only because we
had hassles while moving to a new house."

While things were going well in his personal life,
Duane and William Lee were handling bookings for
the group, which was quite a challenge.

The Oaks were becoming a primary force in gospel
music in the 1970s, one of its most innovative influences. They won numerous Dove Awards from the
Gospel Music Association and several Grammy
Awards. During that time Duane co-authored and
published a book, *The History of Gospel Music*. The
book is no longer in print. But the group's contemporary leanings cost them concert bookings.

"No one but our banker would believe we were
starving to death," Duane says. "The country industry thought we were a big gospel act and didn't need
the country dates.

"There were times when things got pretty tough.
Golden was going through a divorce. His dad bought
him a car, and he was living in the office I owned."

In the early 1970s, William Lee was listed as the
group's manager. Duane was president of the Oaks'
music publishing ventures, Silverline and Goldline
Music, Inc., and president of O.R.B. Productions,
which produced and distributed a radio show hosted
by the Oaks. He also was a partner with the Oaks and
KTAL-TV in Tal-Oak Productions, which produced
and syndicated the Oaks' television show in the late
sixties. He was the owner of Duane Allen Sound,
president of Superior Records, and an owner of
F.A.B. Press, a printing company.

But as their economic fortunes were changing, so
was the group's membership.

Bass singer Noel Fox decided to leave the group in
1972.

"I was really devastated because I loved Noel," Duane says. "The three bass singers that had sung with the Oaks were the best bass singers that have ever been in the business.

"At the time when Noel let us know he was leaving, we had been working with the Stamps Quartet for a year in the Gospel Festival USA. Richard Sterban always impressed me, and during our time in the festival I had lots of talks with Richard. I knew he really liked the Oaks and might consider joining. When Noel left, no one else was really considered. We offered it to Richard."

Likewise, when tenor singer Willie Wynn decided in 1973 to leave the Oaks, Duane says Joe Bonsall was the only person seriously considered. Duane had produced several albums by Joe's group, the Keystones, for Duane's Superior Records.

For Joe and Richard, who had sung together in the Keystones before Richard joined the Stamps, it was heaven on earth. The two friends were working together again in the group they admired the most— The Oak Ridge Boys.

During the tough years, Duane says, several things kept them going.

"We tried to keep cost-of-living raises for everyone, we put new songs in the show to keep it interesting for us, and we kept the bus air-conditioned. There is nothing worse than coming from a show to a hot bus. That caused problems and arguments. With these things, we could be hot on stage, cool on the bus, and keep the bills paid."

Joe and Richard were quickly put to work in areas other than the stage.

"I got Joe to help us with booking some dates, too. He knew the promoters in the Northeast. Richard helped too, but we steered Richard in the direction of disc jockey and press interviews.

"Richard is a really positive person and never has anything bad to say about anybody. With his tremendously low voice, he sounds great on radio interviews.

Disc jockeys really like talking to him. I talk real slow, and I sound awful on the radio. I think Richard is almost solely responsible for all the excellent tour press coverage we've had over the years."

Duane says going through the tough times when everyone had to pitch in and help with various business functions has helped him and the group understand all aspects of their career.

"There was a time when Golden and I were the lowest-paid members of the organization," Duane says. "When we came back from the Soviet Union tour with Roy Clark in 1976, Joe and Richard were making about $300 a week. Two band members were making $225. Golden and I were making $250. The band members said they had to have $50 more a week or they would have to quit. We didn't have it. Golden and I took a $50-a-week cut. We owned the group, and we had the lowest salaries. But it was worth it. We became bigger men for it."

While The Oak Ridge Boys are planted firmly among country's elite, Duane has become recognized within the group and within the music business as being a real student of show business. His onstage look has often reflected a businessman's image.

To Duane every decade had a major influence. "In the late seventies," he says, "it was the movies. Kenny Rogers, Dolly Parton, and Loretta Lynn were either in movies or had films about them. It fueled a real explosion for country music. Country was bigger than ever. When it started down, it went back to where it was before the explosion. Country music is doing well. Every time country reverts to the old sound, it means there is nothing new that is good enough to be a dominant creative force."

There are three ways to make it in the music business, Duane says.

"One is by having hits. Another is being good every time you go out onstage. The third is television. The

Oak Ridge Boys went about it the hard way. We were an institutional advertisement for years. The stage was our ticket. We were on Johnny Carson's 'Tonight Show,' singing 'Just a Little Talk with Jesus' before 'Y'all Come Back Saloon' was ever recorded.

The most important thing in the success formula, Duane says, is a three-minute hit record.

"The second most important thing is another three-minute hit. And the third is another three-minute hit. Hits put people in the seats to see you perform. Maybe they will buy the records. You do television to show people what you look like. As Don Light told me: 'It's amazing how lucky you get the harder you work.' We really did do it the hard way. We had the reputation of being a live act. When the hits came along, we had it all together."

All the years on the road have taught Duane other lessons, too.

"I've learned to get my rest. In the early years, I tried to get as many hours out of the day as I could. Sometimes, I still do that. I think I've become a more confident person and performer, too. I still get butterflies, but it's anticipation and excitement, not fear or nervousness."

Like any music star on the road today, Duane faces any number of temptations. He chooses to ignore them.

"I'm happily married, and I plan to keep it that way," he says. "I see lots of pretty women, but I'm not looking."

The pressures of travel are much easier now, Duane says.

"I have studied the logic and patterns of touring very carefully. People who go in a chain of one-nighters burn themselves and their voices out. They don't finish the tour. You can't string a new vocal cord like you can a new guitar string. You have to rest your voice, or you'll lose it. If you lose it, you disappoint fans and alienate promoters."

The Oaks sang about two hundred concerts in a hundred cities in 1986.

"Touring isn't particularly profitable," Duane says. "If you can break even, you are doing well. Travel costs—especially in the summer—are high. All the hotel rates are at their highest. So is food, fuel, and bus repair."

Still, Duane wouldn't want to be doing anything else.

"The greatest reward of my life is being an Oak Ridge Boy. This career is its own reward. I always wanted to be a group man, not a soloist. This way, we share the applause, the good things, and the hassles. It is a shared thing with us. I feel real good about the Oaks and my role in it. I've been able to do what I want to do with the people I want to do it with.

"The group is magic. We add up to a bigger one than me alone. We've all had hits by singing lead on Oak Ridge Boys records."

None of that would be possible, Duane says, without the devoted support of the Oaks' fans.

"I think we have the best fans in the world. It blows me away how they have stayed with us. That's humbling to the ground to me. When people come to see us, they've got to put gas in the car, there's tickets to buy, and sometimes dinner. They've spent a lot of money to see us. We have always believed in giving our fans more than their money's worth. We like to give them something extra, too. I just want people to believe what they've seen is good—real good."

The biggest price of fame, Duane says, is hassles.

"That's the side of the business no one warns you about. The more popular you get, the more intense the hassles."

Along with singing with the Oaks, Duane is keeping up on other activities. Since he has stepped away from some of the Oaks' administrative work in favor of Joe Bonsall, Duane is finding more time for writing songs.

"For a long time, the most I could do was suggest ideas to our staff writers. Now I'm getting time to write again. That makes me very happy." One of the songs on the *Seasons* album, "Everybody Wins," was co-written by Duane.

Duane also is keeping his production skills honed by working with new artists through his Rockland Roadhouse Productions.

To his friends and partners, Duane is known by his nickname, "Ace."

"That comes from Don Knotts. During an episode of 'The Andy Griffith Show,' he became the owner of a sweater with an *A* on it. He said, 'Call me Ace, I like it.' So did I. The staff gave me a T-shirt with 'Call me Ace' on the front, 'I like it' on the back. I loved it."

Duane also loves to take part in practical jokes. Most of the jokes have their roots in travel.

"We always played jokes. We used to run with the Speers. One night our bus was filled with crickets. We got even. We put 'I Love the Oaks' stickers all over the inside of their bus and filled the bus with empty record boxes. We put crickets in their bus one night in Nebraska. They got even by setting off tear gas in ours."

And while the practical jokes help relieve the monotony and tension associated with travel, that is but one side of Duane's personality. He loves a good laugh as well as the next person. He knows what he wants out of life and knows what it takes to make it meaningful for him.

"My family, my career, and my reputation are important to me. But I have to be at peace with myself before I can make peace with anyone else. I like to base my life on positive results, and then I'll deal with the negatives."

One thing he likes about the Oaks' schedule is the

freedom to do things a lot of people miss.

"I get to go to the PTA, to basketball and football games at our high school, and other things that people with nine-to-five jobs don't get to do. When I'm off the road, I'm off. I'm home. We have a lot more time at home now than we used to."

That leads to the bottom line for Duane. Family. Home. The land. It is his source of stability and serenity. If you were to drive by Duane's farm, you would likely see him driving around on a tractor or doing real hands-on work.

"In the morning, I get up, make coffee, get the mail, and go to the farm and check on my animals. I learned it from Dad. It keeps me in tune with things that have to go on in life. We live in a plastic, rather glitzy world. People have a tendency to put you on a pedestal. As long as you realize that pedestal is anchored to the ground, I think you'll be OK. But when you think it is suspended in the air, your ego becomes bigger than your career.

"The farm keeps me in balance. It's second nature to me. I don't want to be a farmer. My parents did that. They sing because it is fun. I'm just the opposite. My parents were surprised I could make a living this way."

On his farm, Duane has thirty-three head of Texas longhorn cattle, three burros, four horses, a lake stocked with fish, and 150 wild Canadian geese.

"What appeals to me about the farm is there are a lot of animals there that were endangered at one time. We've got Canadian wild geese, Texas Longhorn cattle and burros from Death Valley. I have learned a lot by watching them. All these animals sustain, help each other. It's part of a cycle. It teaches me a lot about patience and keeps me close to the ground. The animals and the farm keep me in contact with things that are not glorified. It helps keep me regulated, in balance. It gives me time to be alone and think. When I get depressed, I have to get it right with myself and with my God. Then I can deal with others."

Duane also finds a great deal of pleasure and relaxation in his classic car collection, which he houses as "Ace on Wheels," a museum that was opened to the public for the first time during Fan Fair in 1986.

"I got my first car nearly twenty years ago. It was a 1931 Model A Ford. I bought it in Texas and towed it home. The next one was a 1926 Model T Ford I bought in Kentucky. I'm from Texas, and Norah Lee is from Kentucky. We call those two our husband-wife team of old cars.

"Norah Lee has bought me cars, pickups, or tractors for the past several years. I've got about twenty-five cars now. I look forward to opening a real museum some day."

Opening the museum for the fans was a real treat, he says.

"It gave me a chance to visit with the fans. We also collected donations for the Humane Society."

Duane's first car has been restored twice. One of the thrills from his childhood involved riding in an old Jeep. Then there was the time when he was thirteen years old and tried to drive a neighbor's car.

"I drove it into the ditch," he says, laughing. "My Dad warmed my britches good when I did that. Now, my son, who is twelve, wants to drive so bad he can hardly stand it. That's the way I was."

Duane, however, still gets into trouble with his driving.

"I've gotten my tractor stuck so many times, it's kind of a joke around home."

Yes, Duane Allen has come a long way from his boyhood on the farm near Taylortown, Texas. He's reached his goals—and exceeded them—many times over.

"Success is determined by three words—pass it along. If you hoard it, it's over. We like to take care of people.

"I was rich before I had money," Duane says. "My mom and dad taught me what rich was when they taught me what love means. My family has been my biggest support, and I'm very grateful for that. I try to show them my appreciation every day I live. When you send love to people, it's like a light that shines from your heart. When people reflect that light back to you, it is the best feeling in the world. I love to shine my light."

Evangelism started creeping in. . . . The Bible thumpers were trying to turn their concerts—that people paid six or eight dollars to see—into church services. People don't want to pay six dollars to go to church. If you don't believe it, you can check the average offering.—Noel Fox, Oak Ridge Boys bass singer, 1968–72.

We were doing it. We were making more money than they were, and we were selling more records, and we had a bigger following and a younger following. And certain groups in the business had quite a bit of jealousy.—Willie Wynn, Oak Ridge Boys tenor singer, 1958–73.

5

CHANGES AND GROWTH: 1965-73

The Oak Ridge Boys immediately put Duane Allen in the spotlight, calling their next album *Duane Allen Out Front*.

Duane had his doubts about filling Smitty Gatlin's shoes and some of the fans agreed. But the Oaks didn't doubt their decision for a moment. As audiences quickly discovered, Duane did not just replace Gatlin, he brought a new and different sound to the group. His formal training showed in his deep, rounded vowel tones and his almost operatic vibrato. (In some of the early recordings, particularly on fast tunes, the training actually seemed to get in the way of his delivery.) He could sing in the smooth style of Gatlin, but he also had a powerful, emotional side that was a contrast to Gatlin's reserved delivery.

There was another difference—more important, though less obvious—between the two lead singers. Smitty Gatlin was, by all accounts, one of the greatest, nicest guys on the face of the earth. But, as Willie

75

Wynn explained, "He had no ambition to go any farther than to just sing pretty. He didn't have that ambition to become a star that everybody else had. Smitty was more involved in being a super-nice guy, and he was totally afraid of hurting anybody or getting on anybody's toes. He just liked to sing good and do a good show, but he didn't have that drive and that foresight and that ambition to become something a whole lot better than we were at the time.

"I think it was the general feeling among everybody that Duane was a go-getter and an asset," Wynn added. "He probably didn't know at that time how much of an asset he would be. Duane was the driving force. Duane definitely made a difference—probably the biggest difference in style and in the changes that brought them where they are today. He had the voice and the direction and the hustle."

Duane's debut album was also the debut for The Oak Ridge Boys on the Heartwarming label. They had offers from two new, all-gospel companies—Heartwarming, based in Nashville, and Word, based in Waco, Texas. They chose Heartwarming, and the relationship prospered right up to the time they left gospel music.

In the spring of 1968, The Oak Ridge Boys reached what was at that time a milestone in gospel music—for the first time, they received $500 for a show.

"I'll never forget it," Herman Harper said. "It was in Charlotte, North Carolina, the Saturday before Easter. That was a certain pinnacle, the $500 show. Once you reached that, you were there."

By the fall of 1968, The Oak Ridge Boys had had the same lineup for close to three years, equaling all previous records for stability. There would only be three more changes. The first came when Harper decided to resign. He was still young—he wouldn't be thirty for another few months—but he had been on the road for almost twelve years, and the "young buck" was now a family man.

"We had just come off a forty-five-day tour of the West Coast," he said. "I had three boys, and I couldn't feature them all growing up and me never seeing them. So I decided I needed to get off the road. Don Light had formed the agency and had asked me to go into business with him. I came off the road and called Don and said, 'Are you ready?' He said, 'No, I was thinking about five years from now, but come on.' That was the last week in September of '68. I couldn't get up enough nerve to tell the guys until the first weekend in November, and I left the first weekend in December. I continued to book them as long as they were in gospel."

To replace Harper, Rex Nelon was considered, but he was already tied up with the LeFevres, so they contacted Noel Fox. Originally from Columbia, Tennessee, an hour south of Nashville, Fox had known the Oaks for years. His first group, the Tennesseans, had bought The Oak Ridge Boys' '60 Chevy station wagon and trailer and had worked shows with them.

"They were the only kind of young group that had been let in the business that Hovie [Lister, of the Statesmen] and J.D. [Sumner, of the Stamps] and James [Blackwood] and all of them had sanctioned," Fox recalled, "and they got all those goody dates."

Fox had had five years of singing experience with the Tennesseans and the Harvesters, but for the last five years he had been working a straight job in Chattanooga, "taking pictures with babies," as Harper put it, for the Olan Mills portrait studio chain. He was as glad to get back into singing as he would be to get out of it five years later.

Fox, like Harper, sang a smooth bass style and was more interested in entertaining audiences than saving them.

"It was just great clean entertainment, and the emphasis was not on the evangelistic side of things," he explained. "We were proud of being involved in a clean sort of entertainment where we could play gymnasiums and schoolhouses and once in a while a nice auditorium instead of a lounge, where people were drunk and bothering you."

As the sixties ended, gospel music was changing fast. The Oaks went on a West Coast tour and found a bunch of hippie-looking Christians who liked their gospel with a rock and roll backbeat. The Oak Ridge Boys, though still basically a southern gospel quartet, were accepted—and, in turn, influenced—by these "Jesus rockers," as they had begun calling themselves.

"There was an energy and youthfulness in the Oak Ridge sound that was really turning them on, really entertaining them," Fox said. "They were having a great time at it.

"We then began—upon the insistence of Bill Golden, who was very style-conscious and liked to look sharp, feel sharp, and dress for success and so on—wearing really, really sharp clothes, you know, those black pin-striped, Edwardian, six-button, double-breasted suits and white turtlenecks."

They might have gotten by with the suits, but turtlenecks were still taboo.

"We were asked to never come back to a Baptist church in Chattanooga, Tennessee, *ever*—the reason being that we dared to appear in a Sunday afternoon concert and a church service that night and we didn't wear neckties," Fox recalled.

"We wore those white turtleneck shirts and appeared, from all they could determine, to be sinners. And they asked us not to ever come back. And we complied, with joy in our hearts."

When it came to being sinful, the Oaks' "worldly" stage clothing was nothing compared to their music. In 1965, Greg Gordon, the fifteen-year-old son of Howard and Anna Gordon of the Chuck Wagon Gang, began appearing onstage with The Oak Ridge Boys, tapping out backbeats on a snare drum. If that was acceptable, it was barely so, and only because the Grand Ole Opry allowed its drummers to use a snare drum (but not a full kit). What followed was not acceptable at all.

In July of 1970, the first International Gospel Song Festival was staged at Nashville's Municipal Auditorium. The two-day extravaganza was a special occasion for the Oaks, since it had been Golden's idea to bring all kinds of gospel acts together in one show, and they worked up something extra for the ten thousand gospel fans who came out to the program. When the Oaks took the stage, Greg Gordon was playing electric bass, and in place of Gordon's snare drum was a full set of drums—cymbals, tom-toms, and everything. And the drummer was not just a guy tapping a brush on a snare. He was Mark Ellerbee from Tallahassee, Florida, a Vietnam veteran and a full-blown rock and roller. He had gotten into gospel because he liked the message, not the pretty music. Ellerbee was one of those Jesus rockers, and he would have a great influence on the music of The Oak Ridge Boys.

"Ellerbee was a real hip drummer and a real good music person," Fox explained. "His head was open musically because he hadn't been raised on four-part harmony or three-chord white gospel. He opened our heads up musically and turned us on to the Andrae Crouch stuff."

Andrae Crouch is black, and his music was to the Oaks of the early seventies what "Dese Bones" and "Go Out to the Program" had been to earlier Oak Ridge groups.

"We worked some dates with Andrae, and we got hooked on the material," Fox said. "I think Duane may have picked the songs, but the overall influence of Andrae came through Ellerbee."

Andrae Crouch's songs carried the gospel message on a standard of high-energy rhythms, joyful choruses, and modern, contemporary melodies and chord changes. It fit right in with the Oaks' approach to music.

"That was some of the highest-caliber audience-moving material that we ever did, I thought," Fox said. "That music had life to it."

But audiences weren't the only ones moving. Part of gospel music, led by Howard and Vestal Goodman, was moving in the opposite direction—away from entertainment and back into the church.

"Evangelism started creeping in," Fox explained. Almost fifteen years after his last appearance on a gospel stage, the thought still infuriates Fox, and he frequently shifts into a sarcastic imitation of a pentecostal preacher when he explains the evangelistic side of the issue.

"Instead of letting the music and the lyrics move people naturally, they began to talk too much and doctrinalize what our little narrow field of entertainment was all about. Howard and Vestal had to be one of the most dynamic acts I've ever seen in my life. They could move an audience. But they insisted on doctrinalizing what they were doing. They almost single-handedly created a divisive force within the business. On the right were the people who were Bible-thumpers and taking their own pentecostal-style interpretation of the Book and applying it to entertainment."

Even though Fox feels strongly that audiences did not want to be preached to, he also believes that some acts used that as a means to get an audience going when their music couldn't.

"I almost feel that it depended on how hard one needed to pull the audience, whether or not *The Lord* got directly involved in the snot-slingings and the blessings," he said. "If the audience was coming along with you and loving you as it was, they'd get up there and cook. But if the audience needs pulling a little, and you had to really get to them hard, they would talk about the Lord in a New York minute. *Talk*—not sing. Talk and shout and call a prayer right in the middle of a forty-five-minute show. As did the Pharisees, I'm told, many years prior."

Despite Duane's nickname during those years— "Preacher," which came from Duane's role as the group's spokesman on stage—the Oaks tried their best to avoid that sort of thing.

"No one in our group felt at all good about trying to move people emotionally with talking and making religious claims and stepping into the areas of doctrine," Fox said. "We'd just have to go ahead and try to get them with music. Duane was always confident in advising the people that music had a sincere message. He'd try to dodge preaching. There were a lot of times when we'd get in a real pentecostal, fundamentalist, traditional-style crowd where they would sit there and be unable to thoroughly enjoy what The Oak Ridge Boys were doing. And if need be, we'd pull 'Go Out to the Program' on them— imitate Howard and Vestal, with Little Willie with his pants rolled up and a skirt on. We could get them with that cornball stuff."

Attacks in the factional war were usually aimed at one of three areas, according to Willie Wynn:

"Long hair, mod clothes, and the contemporary sound. Mainly the people that criticized us, though, were the other groups. A lot of it had to do with jealousy, I do believe. I don't have any other reason for saying that. Most of the other groups in gospel could not have done the type things that we were doing anyway. It'd be like the Kingsmen trying to do an opera. It just wouldn't work. . . . And certain groups in the business had quite a bit of jealousy. Certain ones did not. But you've heard of the Goodmans. And Jim Hammill with the Kingsmen."

The backbiting at times even worked its way onstage, but neither the Oaks nor the Goodmans, who were both managed by Don Light, suffered financially from the controversy.

"We had the biggest grosses in the business at that time, with them on the right and us on the left doing Andrae Crouch material," Fox said, his tone suddenly turning sarcastic, "which, to some groups and promoters, was obviously *sinful* because Andrae Crouch was *black*. He couldn't possibly be Christian or anything like that."

Fox's accusation of racism is not unfounded. He recalled one well-known gospel performer referring to The Oak Ridge Boys' material as "nigger music." And Joe Bonsall remembers an incident at the 1974 Quartet Convention (not long after Joe had joined the Oaks) just before Andrae Crouch's performance.

"One of the biggest promoters at that time was talking to some people backstage," Joe said. "And he told them, 'I am not going to be in the same building with those people,' and he walked out. I saw it first hand, I heard it."

The order in which Willie Wynn listed the criticisms is significant, for of all the controversial topics, *the* most sinful was *not* religion or music, but long hair. Rock stars of the day had hair down to their waists, but in gospel music, "long" hair meant over the collar.

It was such an issue that in 1971, when Duane cowrote and published a book on gospel music, he included two defensive explanations for the new look.

The first came from the Stamps Quartet's bass singer, J. D. Sumner. As a member of the Sunshine Boys from 1948 to 1954, Sumner had made some movies for Columbia studios, and he explained that hair "had to be long for the movies or you'd look as if you didn't have any hair." Of course, few if any gospel acts were actively making movies in 1971, but most were appearing on television, and Sumner said the

TV camera was like the movie camera. In other words, long hair was necessary in order to look normal on TV.

Elsewhere in the book, Duane offered this commentary: "Actually, I recall the first long hair I ever saw on men when I was a boy going to hear gospel groups in Texas. Hovie Lister, J. D. Sumner, and Howard Goodman. That's right, Howard Goodman, though I hear he recently put the Oaks down a little because of their hair. That's OK; everyone has his own opinion."

Then he proceeded with a bizarre explanation of the "long" hair phenomenon: "At that time, hair oil was in style, and between the oil and sweat, sometimes the entire collar of the neck would be ringing wet with oily sweat.

"Then came hair spray. . . . The Oak Ridge Boys, the Prophets, the Statesmen, and eventually about every group kept on wearing it.

"Since the hair was not 'glued' to one's head with oil, it looked as if the hair was longer. Those same people let the hair spray kick die down and are now having a 'heyday' with long hair on groups like The Oak Ridge Boys. . . . It is interesting to note that none of the above groups are singing or living worse or better as the result of wearing longer hair. But, it is also interesting to note that about every group in gospel music has observed more growth in GM [gospel music], both as a business and ministry, in the past three years than ever before in the history of GM."

And there was one other area of sinfulness that, had it been out in the open, might have been devastating to the group.

"I smoked all those years," Fox admits today. "But I would never smoke a cigarette around an audience or even in a dressing room. I would always sneak out to the bus."

That's not the whole story. Fox also drank beer.

"The Oak Ridge Boys almost fired me for bringing beer on the bus," he said. "They knew I was going to drink a beer in the privacy of my hotel room or in the privacy of my home when we were off the road, but never before or even the day of a show."

As Willie suggested, money may have been at the root of the jealousy and finger-pointing. Gospel music was getting bigger and bigger, and the money was getting bigger and bigger, too.

The Gospel Music Association had been formed in 1964, and in 1969, following the lead of the Country Music Association, the GMA started handing out its own awards—the Dove Awards. The first awards underscored the division in gospel music, with Vestal Goodman winning top female vocalist honors and the Imperials, the only group whose progressive attitude equaled that of the Oaks, taking the award for best male group. The Oak Ridge Boys took album of the year honors for *It's Happening*, and their hit single "Jesus Is Coming Soon" was voted song of the year (a songwriter's award).

The next year they won the Dove for best male group, and they received a Grammy nomination for album of the year.

In 1971, the Oaks did not win any Dove Awards, nor did anyone else except the Blackwood Brothers and their friends. It was discovered that the Blackwoods had taken advantage of the Gospel Music Association's membership drive and had signed up a considerable number of new members, all of whom were voting members under the GMA rules (which have since been changed).

The new members recruited by the Blackwoods were encouraged to cast their Dove Award votes for the Blackwoods and, in categories for which they were ineligible, other recommended candidates. They swept the Doves, and although they were technically within the rules, questions of ethics and fairness arose. It was an embarrassing situation for the Blackwoods, and group leader James Blackwood apologized publicly to the gospel music industry and the fans.

The GMA, also embarrassed, invalidated the 1971 Dove Awards. The Oaks did not win a Dove, but they did win one of the more prestigious Grammy Awards that year. In competition against all styles of gospel music, the membership of the National Academy of Recording Arts and Sciences (the Grammy people) voted The Oak Ridge Boys single "Talk About the Good Times" the best gospel performance of the year.

As their awards indicate, The Oak Ridge Boys' reputation was growing. In 1968, the station manager of KTAL-TV in Shreveport, Louisiana, had been so impressed with the audience response at an Oak Ridge Boys concert that he offered them a weekly show. The thirty-minute show, "It's Happening with The Oak Ridge Boys," was taped at the station and syndicated in other markets, and it received a Dove nomination in 1970. One of the show's sponsors was the Downtowner motel company, and the buyer, coincidentally, was Bob Weber, the old piano-jumper from the Oak Ridge Quartet of the fifties.

Duane revived his deejay career, taping a weekly thirty-minute show, "The Oak Ridge Boys with Sounds of Nashville," and syndicating it in fifty or sixty markets.

In 1970, the Oaks made the first of several highly successful tours of Sweden. They were invited by the Samuelson Brothers, a Swedish group that played the Quartet Convention. The Samuelsons wanted to bring an American group to Sweden and the Oaks were invited. It was particularly enjoyable because they were able to get away from gospel music's factional wars.

They were "pleased to find our audience was

mainly comprised of enthusiastic young people," Fox reported in the Oaks' fan club newsletter. "In the USA," he added, "we are required to sing many types of material, including some of the more staple stylings, whereas in Sweden, the more contemporary and modern, the better."

Their international appearances led to the International Gospel Song Festival, which in turn led to a production called Gospel Festival USA. It was a package show that featured the Oaks, J. D. Sumner and the Stamps, and the Singing Rambos. The second half of the program was a religious musical drama, *The Three Nails*, which featured members of all the groups and their bands in the various roles.

The Oak Ridge Boys appeared on "The Tonight Show," performing with Louisiana governor and gospel singer-songwriter Jimmie Davis. In 1971, they starred on a special all-gospel version of Johnny Cash's network TV show. In June of that year, they performed at the Grand Ole Opry on a weekend when all four shows were sold out. They were the only gospel act in the Saturday night show, a move explained by Opry manager Bud Wendell in an article in *Billboard*.

"The Oak Ridge Boys were utilized," the article said, "because of their growing importance in the country field as well as in gospel, where they have won virtually every award in the past year."

They continued their award-winning ways, sweeping the 1972 Dove Awards. They were named top male group, *Light* was album of the year, Tony Brown (who had just replaced Tommy Fairchild on piano) was the top instrumentalist, their *Street Gospel* album won in the cover art category, and Johnny Cash won a Dove for his liner notes on *Light*.

There was, however, another factional source of pressure that began to weigh on the Oaks in the early seventies. Unlike the damnations from the right wing, they could not ignore this one. It wasn't a criticism, actually; it was the increasing popularity of Bill Gaither's style of music—ballads, mostly, with a heavily religious lyric set to contemporary music. Gaither won the first eight Dove Awards for songwriter of the year, and he was no less successful as a performing artist.

"This is the only single act that's ever been in white gospel or Christian music that can go in by themselves and put ten thousand people in a coliseum," Fox said. "So there was definitely an inspirational market that wanted to hear it that way—the same market Billy Graham appeals to. That was a requirement for gospel groups, to do some of the heavy religious songs. And that's what the Oaks did do."

The Oaks' 1974 single of Gaither's "Because He Lives" resulted in one of Gaither's Dove Awards, but according to Fox, they did more of that type of material than they really wanted to.

"They finally cut loose from it and began to do stuff where they could just enjoy singing, put on a great show, do good songs, and they finally became millionaires doing it. They were right all along."

The Oak Ridge Boys weren't quite ready to cut loose from gospel, although they could have.

The band had changed and expanded. Don Breland replaced Gordon on bass in December of 1971. Pianist Tony "Tarzan" Brown left the Stamps and joined The Oak Ridge Boys band. (Fairchild had been billed as part of the Oaks, and the other musicians had come under the heading "backed with"). They had used a guitar player in the late sixties, "Little David" Smith, and in 1972 John Rich, who had been with the Rambos, was hired permanently on electric and steel guitar.

With that band, they were set to go country—or even pop, if they wanted to—but their goals still lay on the frontier of gospel music.

In 1972, "The thought was to make it more contemporary and include country," Fox explained. "Willie started singing 'Mama's Hungry Eyes.' That was a Merle Haggard song. We talked of more rock and more openness in our attitude about songs and music, but I don't think there were any direct plans to change from white gospel. There was more of an attitude of opening the quartet angle up to an eight-person group and having more people singing, more of a troupe doing different things, like 'Oh Happy Day,' getting more people singing on it, that kind of stuff. And advancing musically that way, but not necessarily leaving gospel. And including more songs that were gospel in their content, even though they didn't say 'God' or 'Jesus.' "

In 1972, as the Oaks were getting more and more popular, Noel Fox was getting more and more frustrated.

"My ego couldn't quite handle just being a bass singer," he explained. "It's a support part, and I just kind of grew tired of singing." In addition, he had grown to hate the road. "I was always lost on the road. I am without a home when I'm on the road."

Fox left the group and followed in Herman Harper's footsteps to the Don Light Agency. Later, he became the general manager of The Oak Ridge Boys publishing companies.

"When Noel Fox told us he was leaving, I was really devastated," Duane said. "I loved Noel Fox. I loved Herman Harper's singing. The three bass singers that have sung with The Oak Ridge Boys are the three best bass singers that have ever been in the business, who sing bass the way I like to hear it. And that's a melodic bass singer that can sing a lead, but just in a lower range."

The Oaks knew of one bass singer who would fit into their plans—Richard Sterban. Richard had been a member of the Keystones, based in Buffalo, New

York, a group that had been successful in the Northeast doing a lot of Oak Ridge Boys material. Now he was second bass singer to J. D. Sumner in the Stamps, with whom the Oaks had worked on the Gospel Festival USA shows for the past year.

"I had talked with him enough to learn that he really liked our group and might consider it," Duane said. "There was not really any other person ever considered."

"William Lee called me, and I couldn't believe it," Richard said. "When it sunk in, I couldn't contain myself. I would have jumped through the phone if I could have. I had no hesitation about it."

Less than a year later, the Oaks made another change on the front line—at least the fortieth in their history. But this one was different from all the others.

Willie Wynn had been an Oak Ridge Boy for fifteen years—far longer than anyone in the history of the group. And he was *not* tired of it. He actually liked the road. He liked the music they were doing. He liked the country music that they would be doing in a few years. He didn't have a better offer from anyone in or out of music, and he wasn't looking for one. So why did he leave?

"The Oaks are hustlers," he explained. "Always have been, especially the ones that are in there now. And at that particular time, I had a problem at home because of the fact that we were gone quite a bit and the fact that when we came in off the road we'd go to the office. That's what kept the wheels turning and one of the reasons for their success—doing fan club mailouts, calling deejays, just taking care of the general business that they're able to hire people to do now. All that back then was done by us. Just the general involvement, sometimes, I admit was too much, but that was just the name of the game. It drove a wedge between me and them. If everybody else is busting their butt and I'm not doing it and this continually goes on and I'm caught in the middle, it causes pressures. I suppose I'm probably to blame for allowing it to happen."

On October 8, 1973, Willie resigned from The Oak Ridge Boys, taking about $25,000 in cash as a buyout for his share of the partnership. His marriage failed and he started missing the road and his friends on the road. He joined the Statesmen for a year, but after the Oaks, he said, the Statesmen seemed too old-school. He then formed his own gospel group, the Tennesseans, and is now singing in a country group, Sweetwater.

The Oaks did not have to look far to find a new tenor singer. Duane had the man they wanted—Joe Bonsall—already under contract to his record label. Like Richard, Joe had been a member of the Keystones, and he had for all practical purposes auditioned with the Oaks months before at a show in Jamestown, New York, filling in for Willie at a soundcheck.

"When I heard him sing, I knew he could sing with The Oak Ridge Boys," Duane said. "And Golden really liked Joe because he was really lively and didn't sound like all the other gospel tenors."

Duane had tried to get Joe and the Keystones a contract on both Heartwarming and Word, and failing that, he started his own label, Superior Records, to record the group. By the time Willie quit, Duane had produced several Keystones albums and had had Joe under an individual contract for three years.

The offer from the Oaks couldn't have come at a better time for Joe, with the Keystones breaking up and his wife pregnant. In October of 1973, Joe Bonsall became the tenor singer for The Oak Ridge Boys.

The Oak Ridge Boys—Bill (soon to be William Lee) Golden, Duane Allen, Richard Sterban, and Joe Bonsall—were set for superstardom. With their voices, their band, and their progressive attitude, they could push the outer limits of gospel music and cut across the boundaries into country or even pop. Or so it seemed.

Back in 1954, *Time* magazine had featured the Oak Ridge Quartet in a story about boom times in gospel music. In 1973, it was *Newsweek* that pictured the Oaks—the white suits and dark ties of the fifties now replaced by wide-checked sport coats and open collars—over the caption: " 'The blessing' now comes with a rock beat."

The article, centered around the fourth annual International Gospel Song Festival, noted in the first paragraph the Oaks' penchant for turtlenecks and long hair. Still in the first paragraph it reported, "The Oaks, wincing and shouting about King Jesus [their current hit], prance onstage to electrified instruments much like rock and roll stars."

The similarities to the 1954 national press coverage and to the Oak Ridge Quartet of that time would not, unfortunately, end there. Like the earlier group, the 1973 Oak Ridge Boys would soon be one of the most popular gospel groups and, at the same time, one of the most broke. They would have to leave gospel music to break the historical boom-and-bust pattern.

Richard Sterban is my best friend. He is as solid as a rock. I trust him. He is a good, honest man with a lot of common sense. My life would be awfully empty without him—Joe Bonsall

I am emotional, but I am a person that has a tendency not to show my emotions. I harbor things inside too often.—Richard Sterban

6
RICHARD STERBAN:
MR. BASS MAN

It seems impossible to imagine the fashion plate of The Oak Ridge Boys as anything but a deep-voiced bass singer, whose "oom papa mau mau" vocal hook on the Oaks' #1 smash "Elvira" sets fans screaming every time he sings it.

But Richard Sterban was a boy soprano when he sang his first solo at an Assembly of God church in his hometown of Camden, New Jersey.

"My parents reared me in that church," Sterban says. "I was six years old when I sang my first solo. That experience has never left me. I was very nervous, but being in front of people gave me a stimulation, a real satisfaction. It stuck with me all my life. I think that started my interest in being a performer."

Life at home, Richard says, was happy.

The oldest of three children, Richard Anthony Sterban was born April 24, 1943, in Camden, which is across the Delaware River from Philadelphia. His father, Edward, was an electrician. His mother, Victoria, ran the household and reared Richard, his brother, Joseph, and his sister, Susan.

"Our neighborhood was a typical suburban neighborhood in the Northeast. It was middle-class. We didn't have any slums, but there weren't any really affluent people, either. We were not extremely well off, but I never wanted for anything."

In many respects, Richard was a typical boy. He loved athletics. In junior high school he played baseball, and at Collingswood High School he was on the school's cross-country and track teams.

The Sterban family was a musical one.

"My sister plays the piano and performs with a bell choir at her church," Richard said. "When I come home, I try to time my visits when I can hear her perform. My brother played trombone in the high school band. Mom and Dad also played music— Mother the piano and Dad the accordion."

Richard's father, in fact, had some performing experience.

"When Dad met Mom, he was playing accordion in some local bars and taprooms in the Camden area. Dad is from a Polish family, and Mom is of Italian extraction. But when he met Mom and she got him going to church, he quit the bars."

The church also would play a pivotal role in Sterban's life and his choice of career.

"My parents insisted that I go to church. It wasn't just a matter of Sunday services. There was a youth group and Bible study. I missed out on a lot of school activities I wanted to get involved in because church always had to come first. It was frustrating sometimes, especially when I was a teenager. But, looking back, I really don't regret it. It helped mold my character, and I think that training has a lot to do with my being a fairly disciplined person.

"I always felt music would be a major part in my life. I guess the first turning point of my life was that first public performance as a child. That mixed feeling of being scared and stimulated at the same time, well, that's what makes what we do as the Oaks so worthwhile."

One of his earliest memories as a child was sitting in front of the family television on Saturday night watching "The Lawrence Welk Show" and being fascinated by bass singer Larry Hooper.

Another turning point for Richard came several years later when a relative gave him an album by the Blackwood Brothers for his birthday.

"I was probably nine or ten. I put that record on. J. D. Sumner was singing bass. The sound of those voices singing together, especially the bass voice, appealed to me so much. J.D. really captured my imagination. I wanted to be like him. I went to the record store to try to get more albums. In those days, the Blackwoods were the only gospel group on a major record label."

Through mail order, Richard started collecting gospel quartet music by the Blackwoods, the Statesmen, and other groups. He was fascinated by the traditional four-part southern gospel harmonies.

"I had other influences, too, like the old rock records that featured a prominent bass singer. Some did recitations. That started to grab me, too. I loved Danny and the Juniors. At the time, I thought 'At the Hop' was a great record."

While he was absorbing all these influences, his voice began changing. By the time Richard reached the seventh grade, the former boy soprano was singing tenor in the school's glee club.

"When I came back to the eighth grade, my voice had dropped more than an octave. I was singing bass. Finally, at thirteen, my voice had changed."

What really pushed Richard over the edge and led him to decide on his life's work came when he saw his first professional quartet in person.

"The Couriers were a big influence on me and on

Joe Bonsall, too. I remember the first time they came to our church. I was sitting in the front row. I was captivated every time that bass singer moved. I may have been sixteen years old at the time, because I think I had my driver's license."

When the group announced their next concert was at a church just a few miles away, Richard knew he had to be there.

"I probably would have borrowed the car, but Dad needed it. I got a ride with a friend to the church and sat through their performance once again. I couldn't believe it; I was in heaven. It turned me every way but loose. I hung around those guys after they finished singing. I hit them like a lot of our fans hit the Oaks today. I wanted to know everything. I asked them everything I could think of, especially the bass singer. Before I knew it, they had all their equipment packed up, loaded it, and they were gone."

Richard suddenly realized that not only was he there alone; it also was raining, and he didn't have a ride home.

"There I was, standing in the parking lot without a way to get home. I didn't care. I walked home in the rain. I had bought one of the Couriers' albums, and I kept it under my coat. By the time I got home, I was soaked and the album cover was ruined. But I couldn't wait to play the record. I still have it.

"But that was it. From that night on, I knew what I wanted. I wanted to sing in a quartet."

So, at the age of sixteen, the course of Richard's life was set.

The Couriers pioneered gospel singing in the Northeast. They also promoted gospel concerts in the area around Trenton and Philadelphia. At one of those concerts, Richard heard The Oak Ridge Boys.

"Herman Harper was singing bass for the Oaks then. They had a rickety old broken-down bus. They were struggling, but I loved what they did. I knew then I wanted to be a part of the Oaks."

After graduating from high school, he enrolled at Trenton State College with plans to study music. But he had to pass a test first.

"I went for my interview with the president of the college before I was officially accepted. We talked about my ambitions and interests. At the time, I thought I would be a performer. I also thought about a career in opera. The president had a low voice, too. He asked me to sing a low C. I did. I was accepted. I never studied opera, but it was a fascination. I used to listen to opera more than I do now."

While he was studying at Trenton State, Richard met three young singers from Pennsylvania who shared his passion for quartet singing. Together they formed the Keystone Quartet.

"We sang in churches, at revivals and camp meetings around Pennsylvania and New Jersey. We were all members of the Assembly of God Church. I took some correspondence courses from the church's Bible college. I had a minister's license for a while. Actually, it was the first stage of ministry in the church. I had an exhorter's permit. I couldn't perform marriages. When we were asked to sing, we also were expected to convey a message, to give an invitation at our program. A basic knowledge of the Bible and of church doctrine was necessary."

One of the places the Keystones sang during 1963 was Ardmore Junior High School in Philadelphia. They were on the same program with the Happy Goodman Family, the Blackwood Brothers, the Statesmen, and the Couriers.

In the audience that night was a then fifteen-year-old Joe Bonsall, who was moved by what he saw and heard.

"I thought Richard was really cool," Bonsall recalled.

But Richard and Joe didn't meet that night.

Joe, who was singing in his own quartet, the Faith Four, also booked other quartets into churches with his own.

When the Keystones went their separate ways, Richard joined the Eastman Quartet. The Eastmans worked on several programs with the Faith Four, and Joe and Richard became friends.

"I was working for Gimbel's Department Store, selling men's clothing," Richard remembers. "Joe was always coming by to talk quartets. It was a real passion for both of us."

It was at one of those Philadelphia concerts that Richard finally met his idol, J. D. Sumner.

"He really is one of my heroes," Richard says. "I was really very nervous when we met. I asked him for advice on being a bass singer. He said, 'Son, drink coffee, lots of it, and drink it black.' He was putting me on, of course, but I didn't take any chances. Later, he took me under his wing and was very helpful to me."

Another passion also began to take hold while Richard was working at Gimbel's—fashion.

"I read all the fashion magazines, hung around the store's buyers, and asked lots of questions. I couldn't seem to learn enough fast enough."

The roots of Richard's interest in fashion, like his music, began at home.

"My parents were real sticklers about my appearance. We bought quality at home, not quantity. I guess my interest in fashion always has been with me."

Richard's personal life hit a high note in 1964 when he married his childhood sweetheart, Sandra.

"We went to the same church. She is a very religious person." Their first child, Richard, was born a year later. The next year, Doug was born. Their third son, Christopher, was born in 1970.

The marriage would end in divorce in the early

eighties after a separation of a year-and-a-half.

"There is no question about it—my marriage was a casualty of my career. I would be the first to admit it. My being gone constantly played a major role in that."

After Richard and Sandra were married, the Keystone Quartet was re-formed and Richard was, once again, singing bass in the group. A year later, Joe Bonsall left his struggling Faith Four Quartet to join Richard in the Keystones as the tenor singer.

"It was a real hand-to-mouth existence. We weren't exactly getting rich," Richard recalls. "But it was wonderful, too. We were happy to sing. We got to sing with some great groups, and I learned so much."

After a time, the Keystones left their home base of New Jersey and Pennsylvania and moved to Buffalo, New York.

"We set up a business booking other gospel groups into the area. We sang on the shows, too."

One of the acts booked into the area by the group was The Oak Ridge Boys, whose lineup by this time included William Lee Golden and Duane Allen. The Oaks and the Keystones formed a close friendship, and the Oaks reciprocated bookings, giving the Keystones a chance to expand their performing horizons to the large gospel festivals in the South.

"The Oaks were very innovative," Richard recalled. "They used a rock band, wore the current fashions of the day, and had longer hair."

The Keystones' friendship with the Oaks continued to blossom. When Duane Allen started his independent gospel music record label, Superior Records, the Keystones recorded several albums with Allen as the producer.

That didn't mean the Keystones were rolling in the proverbial clover. The gospel music industry wasn't oriented to concerts and tickets. For many acts, such as the Keystones, and even gospel's top headliners,

love offerings were a way of life. When you are a
family man with three children, love offerings di-
vided four ways often weren't enough to keep things
going.

"I was married and had three boys to support. I
wasn't making much of a living with the Keystone
Quartet."

When J. D. Sumner called Richard and asked him
to take his spot in the Stamps Quartet, it was an offer
he couldn't refuse. Shortly after he joined, the
Stamps began backing Elvis Presley. Richard
packed his wife and children, and the Sterbans
moved to Nashville.

Suddenly Richard was thrust from singing for a
handful of people for love offerings at churches and
revivals to singing before thousands of screaming
fans with the king of rock and roll at Las Vegas and
in concert halls around the world.

It was a heady time for Richard that brought an
end to his financial problems but started new problems at home.

"We started to have difficulties when I departed
from singing gospel and began singing country. I
think the real division came when I joined the
Stamps and started singing with Elvis. My wife was
not in favor of that. We started doing songs like 'Help
Me Make It Through the Night' and songs that talked
about cheating and so forth. She asked me how I
could sing lyrics like that. At that point, she became
very critical of my career. That's when we started
growing apart."

For his career, though, the time with Elvis was a
dream come true.

"I used to dream about something like that. And it
was coming true. Elvis always wanted me and J. D.
close to him on the stage so we could sing the bass
parts in his ear."

Richard credits Presley and the Stamps for helping prepare him for the massive popularity that would come later with the Oaks.

"I think I'm a better professional person for having been with Elvis and the Stamps. I have tried to observe other successful people. I've learned what to do and what not to do."

While Richard and his wife were growing apart, he and Joe Bonsall stayed close in touch. The Keystones were going on without a bass singer.

"I auditioned a lot of bass singers, but I never found one I liked," Joe says. "We sang as a trio."

When the Stamps weren't working with Elvis, they played gospel concerts, revivals, and at some churches. On some of those dates, they worked with The Oak Ridge Boys.

In 1972, bass singer Noel Fox left the Oaks and Richard was offered the job. He accepted enthusiastically, though to many, it looked as if Richard was taking several steps backward. He was turning his back on a lucrative spot with the most popular man in rock and roll history to join a group with no following outside of gospel music.

"I really thought that, of all the gospel groups in the business, the Oaks had the most potential. It was the best decision I ever made."

And now, with The Oak Ridge Boys, Richard has played many of the same arenas and concert halls he played with Elvis. And, like Presley, he has seen them filled to capacity.

"When I was a boy, I wanted to be part of the best vocal group in the world. I am part of one of the best; there is no doubt about that."

But before Richard would see his faith in the Oaks become reality, The Oak Ridge Boys would have to face some tough times of their own.

"We had our lean years," Richard says. "We really did struggle and wondered if we were going to survive. Financially, things were pretty tough. But I never lost faith in the group. I really felt that, if we could just hang in there, we would make it."

Through those lean years, when the Oaks' progressive musical and fashion styles stirred controversy in the gospel music industry, the Oaks had friends helping them out.

"Johnny Cash helped us survive. He believed in us, inspired us to go on. Then came Roy Clark and Jim Halsey."

In 1977, the Oaks made their move to country music with a record Richard still considers one of their best—"Y'all Come Back Saloon."

And finally, the times began to get better. The Oaks began making the transition from gospel to country, from near bankruptcy to material comfort.

Just as the Oaks were starting to roll, tragedy struck Richard head-on. His father died of a heart attack in 1978. He was in the Oaks' recording studio with Joe Bonsall, doing a radio interview. He remembers that day all too vividly.

"One of our secretaries came into the studio and handed me a message to call my uncle. I thought I would wait until the interview was over. She came back in again, and we decided to cut the interview short. I knew it must be something serious, but I never suspected anything. I was on my way back to my office when Duane intercepted me. He told me what had happened. It was a shock. It was very unexpected. I had seen him just a few weeks before, and he looked tired but didn't appear to be ill. I couldn't dial the telephone. Duane called for me, and I talked to my uncle.

"Dad had a heart attack on the way to work. It was on a Monday morning, right after the Super Bowl on Sunday. He and the guys who rode to work with him were discussing the game. Dad was driving. They got into the parking lot, and Dad just slumped over. I had a few days off and flew home so I could be with Mom and my family. Then the Philadelphia airport got snowed in. We had a concert on Friday in St. Louis, and I couldn't get there. It was the only Oaks concert I've ever missed."

Hard work and a busy schedule helped Richard cope with his loss.

"We were so busy I didn't have a lot of time on my hands. That helped."

For his mother, however, the loss was devastating.

"Dad was the center of her life. She had never paid bills or dealt with business at all. She had a hard adjustment. For years, she wouldn't allow herself to enjoy life. It was especially tough during holidays, anniversaries, and birthdays. She's loosened up a lot now. She's enjoying life, and she is dating."

Richard's marriage began to reach a breaking point in 1981 as well. After a separation of a year-and-a-half, they were divorced.

"My former wife is a good person. I don't hold any grudge toward her. I don't feel I love her anymore. It is the best thing we are no longer together. Even now, though, I have a bad day and feel some hurt over it. And it hit me heavily financially."

Richard's ready admission that his failed marriage was a casualty of his career has added to the guilt many divorced people have felt.

"I felt I wasn't a successful husband, I wasn't a successful father. I worried about how my kids would perceive me. My divorce is the greatest price of my success."

Love has been a rocky road for the dark-haired, deep-voiced singer. And that includes his current relationship with travel agent Donna Summers.

"Donna is my lady. I met her at George Lindsey's golf tournament in Montgomery, Alabama. She was a member of a group of women called the Crewmates, who represent the state at various events. We had to ride a float together in a parade. It was a big old battleship. We stood kind of next to each other. She is very shy, and so am I. We hardly spoke to each other."

They did, of course, get together. In time, she moved to Tennessee. And they almost were married on February 4, 1983.

"It was the day of the wedding when I backed out," Richard says. "I couldn't sleep at all the night before. I pictured myself walking down the aisle, taking those vows again. I couldn't do it. I just couldn't do it. I could see the looks on the faces of my mom and my kids. It just didn't seem right. I felt if I had married Donna that day it would have affected my relationship with my boys. It was just too soon. So I left. I just couldn't face anyone right then.

"Donna is a very special person, and the last thing I wanted to do was hurt her. But, at the time, I didn't see any other way around it. It was very traumatic for both of us."

Trauma turned to anger when Richard saw an article in a Knoxville, Tennessee, newspaper.

The headline, Richard recalls, said, "Richard Sterban Leaves Donna Summer at the Altar."

"They ran a picture of me and a picture of Donna Summer [the pop/disco singer] with the story. When I read it, my first reaction was 'My God, when people get hold of this, it could not only affect my career, but that of my three partners.' Unfortunately, some country music fans seem to have some prejudice against black people. I called our publicist, Kathy Gangwisch. She got in touch with Donna Summer's people to assure them we had nothing to do with that story. There was no problem on their end.

"I got to thinking that maybe I could sue the paper, but I realized that the Oaks would want to play Knoxville again someday. We'll want their help to support our show. What good is it going to do to sue the paper and have them turn against us? I dropped the idea and asked them to please be more careful in the future."

After Richard returned home, a very hurt Donna Summers called and asked if she could see him.

"We talked about it, why it happened. She told me there was no reason we couldn't be friends. She really impressed me. She gave me back the engagement ring and said it meant nothing to her if we weren't married."

Richard ponders the question of whether he is afraid to get married again.

"I think I was afraid to get married at that time. Ultimately, I think I will. I guess there is some fear there. Having gone through a divorce, I made a vow to myself I would never experience that again. It is very traumatic.

"Maybe I yet don't believe I can be totally 100 percent faithful to one person. When I come to that realization, maybe then I will get married. I'm not implying I'm unfaithful to Donna. I'm not out messing around with a different woman every night. Mentally and emotionally, in a lot of ways, I feel like I'm totally locked in to the point I can make this lady the main thing in my life. For a marriage to be a success, it has to be that way."

While Donna maintains her own apartment, she naturally spends a lot of her time at Richard's Hendersonville home.

"Donna gets along very well with my boys. I think we're getting closer to marriage all the time. I've got about another year of heavy obligations to my ex-wife to go. I'd like to get that behind me before I marry."

This time, Richard believes it will work.

"Look what we've already been through together. One of the reasons I think we'll last is because we've survived that hurdle of not getting married once before."

Along with conquering his fear of love, Richard

also is winning another battle with a demon that has plagued his professional career.

"The biggest challenge I've faced personally is my shyness. I've always been very shy and quiet. In the early stages of my career, getting on a stage was very stimulating, but I also experienced a great deal of stage fright. One of the most difficult things I had to learn was to relax onstage and be myself. I enjoyed being onstage, but not to its fullest. Learning to walk onstage like I was walking from one room to another was one of the most difficult hurdles I've had to deal with. When we started working on television, I used to think I would pass out. Now I can't wait. I really look forward to it. It's anticipation, not nervousness."

By learning to relax on stage, Richard has begun to do the kind of bass singing he is proud of.

"J. D. Sumner told me I wouldn't do any bass singing worth writing home about until I turned forty. Now I can hear a lot more fullness in my voice. I'm a lot more confident and relaxed when I sing, so my vocal cords get loosened up. A bass voice is like a fine wine. It gets better with age. And I'm coming into my vintage years."

Sumner taught Richard about the psychology of singing.

"He told me there was a little man in my head trying to tell me I couldn't hit that note. You have to convince yourself he's wrong. He has been like a father to me."

Along with perfecting his low notes, Richard has pursued his love of fashion and is known as the most fashion-conscious of the Oaks.

"My goal is to get on a best-dressed list. I could also see myself modeling. Someday, a possibility for the future might be endorsing a line of clothes. I also would love to have my own spread in *Gentleman's Quarterly* or another well-known fashion magazine.

"The fashion business is political too, just like the

music business. I'm hanging around fashion people in New York. To get on one of those best-dressed lists, it's who you know."

Richard has enlisted the advice and support of a former *GQ* editor, Pieter O'Brien. Today, O'Brien is executive vice president of the Henry Grethel Company.

"He is helping me with my image. I have learned so much about myself and clothes from Pieter. I used to feel like I was a little behind the times. I needed a change."

Some of the changes have been dramatic. While Richard was always the Oak you could count on seeing in a perfectly tailored suit and tie, he has become more adventurous. From fancy furs to oversized tuxedo jackets with padded shoulders, Richard's unique wardrobe is making country music audiences sit up and take notice.

Where Richard once wore his hair over the top of his earlobes, he now has it carefully cut above the ear.

Other changes are more subtle.

"Pieter took me shopping and taught me how to shop, how to buy, and how to wear clothes."

His eye-catching apparel has paid some healthy dividends.

"It has done wonders for me in a lot of ways. It has given me a new outlook on myself. I am performing better because I feel better about myself. I feel more free, more energetic. When people pay their hard-earned money for a ticket to see us, I want to go out there and look my best for them, feel my best, and sing my best. I have always felt very strongly about that."

When it comes time to relax, though, Richard is likely to be wearing one of the authentic satin warm-up jackets of professional sports teams he has collected. But even at his most casual, he never loses a sense of style.

Richard's sense of fashion and deep voice also have given him the reputation of being a sex symbol. A survey of readers of *The Music City News* placed him in the Top Ten sexiest men in country music.

"I think a lot of that has to do with my voice as much as anything. Women seem to respond to a low voice. But name the approach, and it's been tried by women in the audience. I've gotten room keys and notes. Some will ask me to join them for a drink. Some get very clever; a few have gotten vulgar and very graphic.

"I'm a normal man. There was a time in my career that I took advantage of those offers. After a while, though, it does get old. It really does. The one-night stand has gotten very old. I only had one girl accuse me of being the father of her baby. I wasn't, but we still had to do blood tests, which proved I wasn't."

Playgirl magazine once approached Richard about an interview.

"I decided not to do it because of the group and the image. I am, honestly, a modest person. I'm reluctant to even go outside with my shirt off."

Being a sex symbol has its dark side, too.

"One girl keeps driving by my house all the time. Another woman threw water on me at the Grammy Awards because I was with Donna. That hurts. Maybe it's because I'm the only single one in the group. With some people there is just no middle ground. They want to be close, but you have to be careful. The vast majority of our fans are so nice, so loyal, so faithful. I love them and appreciate their support so very much."

Richard handles the pressure of life on the road by running several miles every day. It isn't always convenient to do that, but Richard says physical fitness also helps his voice.

"I am convinced that my physical activity has helped me hit even lower notes. I feel I am coming into the best singing and performing years of my life."

The resourceful Sterban finds other ways to cope as well.

"If I can have some time alone, I can deal with anything that comes my way."

Team sports are another passion of Richard's. One of his dreams is to own a piece of a major league baseball team. He already is a partner in three minor league teams.

"In many ways I'm a frustrated athlete. I realized when I was a boy that I didn't really have any talent in that area. Running is the one thing I could do. I realized my talents were in music and stayed with it. I love to watch sports on television, especially baseball."

Life as an Oak Ridge Boy has been rewarding on many fronts.

"We have gotten closer in the respect that we know each other so well. We can almost tell what each other is thinking at a particular time. We can read each other pretty well. We really are closer than brothers."

When William Lee Golden made his much publicized embrace of the mountain man lifestyle, Richard said it caused him great concern.

"I thought his change would harm us, but I was wrong. I think it's a big plus for us. I apologized to him. Sometimes, he didn't communicate his feelings to us."

Richard calls William Lee "one of the most unusual people I know. He also is one of the most sincere. That is one of the reasons he is so well liked by our fans. His voice possesses a sincerity that draws people to him. He is very unselfish."

Being an Oak Ridge Boy is the ultimate, Richard says.

"It's a feeling money can't buy. My ambition from the first was to be part of the greatest vocal group in the world. I want to be remembered as a great singer who made a contribution to the music business and made people happy. When I see our name on a sign or marquee, I feel a sense of accomplishment. I'm very proud of that."

How could Richard handle being apart from the group?

"At first, it would be very difficult to handle. It's much like a major league baseball player retiring. Some adjust well; others have a difficult time. I would like to think that I could handle it well. I hope I'll be in the position of not having to worry about being out of a job."

If he wasn't an Oak Ridge Boy, Richard thinks there would be several career options open to him.

"I would probably be involved in sports. I had offers to get involved in radio, and I think I would have liked being a sportscaster. Or, maybe getting involved on the executive end of baseball. Another field, of course, would be fashion. But the day I am no longer an Oak Ridge Boy would be a very sad day."

There are times Richard says he misses being part of gospel music.

"One of those times happened the night I went to see the Masters V—they really are the superstars of gospel. They called me up to sing 'Just a Little Talk with Jesus' with them. What an experience that was . . . singing with James Blackwood, Hovie Lister, Jake Hess, J. D. Sumner. Someday, I think the Oaks will do another gospel album."

Richard Sterban has seen the dreams of his childhood become reality and then some. His confidence in his future and in himself as a man is growing stronger every day. And while Richard still sees himself as shy, he is aware of a changing self-image.

"I think I am more outgoing now. I think my shyness has been misinterpreted by some people as being stuck up.

"I'm an emotional person, but a person that has a tendency not to show my emotions. I harbor things inside me too often. I take a lot of pride in my appearance, and I try to keep it in perspective. In this business, you have to have self-confidence that borders on conceit. I think I have become a very confident person. I know who I am and where I'm going."

Joe Bonsall is the most energetic, exciting, predictable person I know. I see so many traits in him I hope I can show to others. He is very smart and has a very underrated opinion of himself.—
Duane Allen

*Joe is my best friend. He is the person who, no matter how down and out you may be, has this tendency to make you feel happy, lift you up. He is very compassionate. He's the real energy, driving force in the group.—*Richard Sterban

7

JOE BONSALL:

FROM STREET HOOD TO CENTER STAGE

Lying in the back seat of the '51 Chevrolet, a bruised and bleeding fourteen-year-old Joe Bonsall decided he needed to make some changes in his life.

He and the other members of the K&A Gang had been in a rumble with some other street toughs in his working-class Philadelphia neighborhood. And the skinny little teen-ager had caught the worst of it.

"I got out of the back of the car and got kicked square in the forehead. I fell back in the car and shut the door. I laid on the floor and cried. I was hurtin' something awful."

A voice came through loud and clear, and for once, Joe listened.

"It told me, 'This ain't for you, man; life is bigger than this.' I changed from that night. I asked myself, 'Is this really fun?' The answer was 'Hell, no.' I needed something else in my life. I needed to sing."

It was not the first—or last—time Joe would hear that voice.

113

Joseph Sloan Bonsall was born May 18, 1948, in Philadelphia. His father, J.S., was an electrician. His mother, Lillie, also worked. His sister, Nancy, was born five years later.

"Dad met my mom in the Army during World War II," Joe says. "She was a WAC. Her job was to escort the dead and wounded home from the front. Dad got shot up about forty days after the Normandy landing. There were three machine gun nests shooting at him. He ran out and blew up all three of them. He was awarded the Silver Star. Mom escorted him back home. He spent a couple of years in and out of Veterans Administration hospitals before they got married."

Joe's neighborhood was located in North Philadelphia, an area near the intersection of Kensington and Allegheny avenues, which gave the neighborhood and the gang its name, the K&A.

"There were lots of people in the inner-city neighborhood. At times, I really enjoyed it. There were lots of kids around, and there was a lot to do. People didn't have a whole lot of money. I don't remember it looking as bad as it does now.

"When I was a kid, there were horses and wagons on the street with vendors selling fruits and vegetables. The neighbors seemed close. There were trolley cars running, and you didn't have to go too far from the house to catch one."

Both of Joe's parents worked, but Joe was never alone. Besides the kids in the neighborhood, he had Nana.

"We had this woman living with us. Her name was Gertrude Clark. She was my nanny. We called her Nana. She raised me from age two. Nana loved me to death, and I loved her to death. She was a crusty older woman. I was her pride and joy."

Despite frequent bouts with bronchial asthma as a child, Joe led an active life. The biggest thrill for the kids in his neighborhood was the day one of the guys got a new baseball.

"I played a lot of baseball as a kid. That was all I would do in the summertime. We had a park across from the house. It had the only trees I ever saw as a kid. I'd get up and play all day until it was time for lunch and dinner, then play until it was too dark.

"We only had one baseball among the twelve or so of us guys. We all played with it for ages. If it rolled into the sewer, we had these things made out of hangers to retrieve it, or we'd dump the smallest guy, hold him head first in the sewer to get the ball. We'd let it dry out and play with it some more. If the cover fell off, we wrapped it with electrical tape. We played with it until you could not play with it anymore. The only thrill bigger than a new baseball was a new glove."

Music also was a driving force in his childhood.

"I was a real hamburger," Joe says. "I was always singing. My mother would have company, and she'd say 'Sing something, Joey.' I always did."

At age four, Joe was entered in his first talent contest. He lost but got to be on television.

"That was great. I loved it."

So did Nana Clark.

"I sang gospel, rock, anything she wanted to hear," Joe said. "I sang for anyone at the drop of a hat. I was even doing my kicks when I sang back then. Nana liked the way I sang."

At Webster Elementary School, there was one constant on Joe Bonsall's report cards: "Joey talks too much."

"I talked all the time. I saw my sixth-grade teacher, Miss Caputo, last year. It was neat. She uses me as an example of applying myself and succeeding. But I remember her notes on my report card—'Joey does not apply himself.'

"I guess I didn't as a kid. I wanted to play baseball;

I wanted to be a rock and roll star."

That passion for music was fueled by Elvis Presley.

"I was freaked out with music after I saw Elvis on TV."

Through his childhood, Joe also had to deal with his father's drinking problem, which was caused by his experiences in World War II.

"Dad never talked about the war unless he got a little drunk. He'd always grab hold of me, and he'd tell me how awful the war was, and he promised me I would never go. 'They will never take my son,' he told me. Dad believed there would be another war because it is the nature of men to fight.

"Dad didn't feel like he was a hero just because he had a Silver Star. 'I was a street kid that was angry,' Dad told me. 'I was nineteen years old. I was mad because the enemy had us pinned down. That's why I did what I did. They had killed my friends.' "

The story brings tears to Joe's eyes as the childhood memory floods him. "Dad was a good man. He worked very hard for us. But he did have a bit of a problem with drinking."

Nana was the great stabilizing force in Joe's life.

"She was a powerful force in our family. If Dad came home drunk, he and Mom would fight. Nana could always fix it. She was always there, and she always made sense. We all listened to her and loved her."

One of the biggest traumas of Joe's life came at age eleven, when his beloved Nana died from cancer.

"Before she died, Nana told me I was going to be a big success at whatever I wanted to do. She always told me she would throw me a star. I went to see her in the hospital. She wasn't the same, but she called me to her, told me she loved me."

After Nana died, Joe was hospitalized for his recurring bronchial asthma and was having a bad time.

"One night I was laying in bed, and this light came

into my room to the bottom of my bed. Nana was there. She was in the same color blue they buried her in. She told me she loved me and that she would throw me a star. She told me not to worry.

"I got all excited and told everybody that Nana had been to see me. The doctor told me it was probably a nurse checking in with a flashlight and that the rest probably was a dream. Maybe it was, but every time I see The Oak Ridge Boys' name somewhere, I think of Nana throwing me a star. A lot of good things have happened to me and the Oaks over the years. I've often thought of Nana. I always figure she's there. My Mama thinks she still watches over her. God comes in different forms. Nana was such a powerful influence on our lives."

After Nana's death, Joe's life took several turns—some for the worse.

"I was a skinny little kid in junior high school, and I got beat up a lot. I didn't play as much baseball; I played more rock and roll. I fell away from church and in with some of the worst people I could be in with. I was one of the youngest guys in the K&A gang. They were rough dudes. You had to be a big shot all the time. We dressed up in tight pants, white shirt with tab collar, greased our hair back, and walked around the streets and did our best to be cool. When that got boring, we hung out at the corner. When that got boring, we jumped into a car and went to beat up people.

"Sometimes the knives came out. Usually, the bigger kids took them away. Then the cops would come. I was twelve years old when I joined. I was a tough kid. I walked one-and-one-half miles a day from junior high. No matter how I tried to get out of his way, this one guy always found me and beat me up. There were a couple of times I got revenge. Now it doesn't seem like a big deal. Then it was."

Needless to say, Joe's grades during those turbulent years weren't too good either.

"I finally learned I couldn't live that way anymore."

That fateful night that left Joe battered and bleeding in the back of the '51 Chevy would prove to be a turning point. And music would be his ticket out of a dead-end lifestyle.

"There were some Christian kids in the neighborhood who kept asking me to go to gospel concerts with them. They told me about the gospel quartets. I turned them down for a year. I didn't want the guys to think I was a sissy."

Now, however, Joe was ready. He had left the K&A Gang behind him. It also didn't hurt that the guy driving Joe and the others to the concert had a '61 Buick.

"I thought it was cool to ride in that car. That got me out to see the Couriers and the Blackwood Brothers. That did it. I was hooked. The four voices and piano really freaked me out. I knew right then I wanted to sing in a quartet.

"I had always loved group singing. I heard it in church, and I heard it in groups like the Drifters. I used to sing in the bathtub when I was a kid to get that sound. But the quartet sound I heard that night, the power harmony, blew me down."

Joe had another reason to pursue singing. He couldn't make the football team. He was one of two thousand boys who turned out for varsity football. It took Joe three days to realize he couldn't make it. The former all-star in the Pop Warner league couldn't make it in a league without weight limits. There was one solution.

"I tried out for the choir. I went to Robert Hamilton, who still directs the all-city boys' choir in Philadelphia. I tried out, and I made it. I've been singing ever since."

In addition to school, Joe worked two jobs. One was

for Dr. Frederick Rude, a veterinarian; the other as a short order cook for Betty's Luncheonette.

"Betty told me I could eat all I wanted, and I did. It's a wonder she made any money while I was working there. Somebody would order two hamburgers; I'd fix three and eat one."

In the tenth grade and finally out of the K&A Gang, Joe set about getting the rest of his life in order.

"I also started going to church again. I needed something in my life, and the Lord was a great answer."

Just as things were starting to go right for Joe, a shattering tragedy struck the Bonsall family. Joe's dad was paralyzed by a crippling stroke.

"Dad was working at the time, and we believe an electrical shock might have triggered the stroke. I was working at the veterinarian's that day, and Dr. Rude drove me to the hospital. Dad's right side was completely gone. It took his speech and caused permanent brain damage. He spent several years in the hospital and in rehabilitation centers." Mr. Bonsall has regained some of his mobility but has been confined to a wheelchair for more than twenty years.

The upheaval meant Joe was now the head of the family.

"I had to change everything in my life. God and singing were very important to me, but I had to work to bring home food. I had to grow up fast. I was the head of the family."

There also was an irony to his father's stroke.

"His stroke kept me from having to go to Vietnam," Joe says. "He had promised me when I was a child that I would never go to war, that they would have to take him first. In essence, he kept his word. I didn't have to go."

Joe continued to work for the veterinarian through his high school years and sang in the school's choir.

"One year we raised $80,000 and went on a tour of Scandinavia. Choir was wonderful. I was always yanking kids out of the choir to form quartets. I taught myself some chords on the piano and thumb-slapped it in the old gospel quartet style. I'd get those kids to sing gospel quartet songs."

Despite his new attitudes toward life, Joe still wasn't setting the academic world on fire.

"I wasn't that smart in school. It isn't that I wasn't intelligent; I was just into singing—period. I switched from an academic to a general degree. That gave me time to take lots of music harmony and theory classes. I loved those. When I was in geometry, I drew pictures of buses, microphones, stages, and guitars. I set a course on singing, and I never wa-vered. I knew I would do whatever it took."

After graduation, Joe went to work as a mail boy at a tool company. He worked there for about a year. By then he was singing with his friend Ronnie Graeff, and the two formed the Faith Four Quartet.

"We were terrible, but we had a blast!" Joe said. "I would book the group and other groups around south New Jersey. We had a great time."

Joe switched jobs, this time becoming a mail boy for a sugar company. Soon he was promoted to the sales department.

"I talked to sugar brokers all day. It was fast-paced, and I loved it. I was there a couple of years, but all I thought about—all that mattered to me—was singing."

One of the groups Joe booked was the Eastman Quartet, which featured Richard Sterban as the bass singer.

"I first heard Richard sing when he was with the Keystone Quartet. I was fifteen, and they were sing-ing at Ardmore Junior High School on a program with the Couriers, Happy Goodman Family, Black-woods, Keystones, and The Oak Ridge Boys. The

Oaks were great. Richard, I thought, was really cool."

Richard left the Eastmans to join a re-formed Keystone Quartet. By then, Richard and Joe were close friends.

"Richard was working for Gimbel's then. He was the only other guy I knew who loved quartet singing as much as me. I used to follow him all over Gimbel's while he sold men's clothes and we talked quartets. Besides, he was a bass singer. That was so cool."

The Faith Four began going through changes. Two of the guys were drafted, but Joe kept things going. His sister Nancy sang in the group for a while.

Richard was happy with the Keystones and, just after Joe's nineteenth birthday, the group invited him to join as their tenor singer.

"Richard was quitting Gimbel's to go full-time with the Keystones. They offered me the job, and I took it. They promised me $75 a week, which was less than I was making at the sugar company. I made that salary *maybe* once a month."

The Keystones sang all around the Midwest and the North at youth rallies, churches, and gospel concerts. They barely made ends meet.

"It was a big thing for me to leave home at age nineteen to tour. But I had to do it. Mom was very supportive. She understood."

During a trip through Pennsylvania, the Keystones stopped in a small town to sing at a theater and a church. It was there that Joe met his first wife, Barbara. Her father owned the theater where the group sang, and they sang at Barbara's family's church.

"Before I was married, I lived on our bus for six months. I didn't mind that much. I had my car; I was singing. That was all that mattered. I slept a lot in that car."

Barbara and Joe were married in 1969 and had

barely finished their honeymoon when the Keystones packed up and moved to Buffalo, New York.

Things didn't look much better for the Keystones in Buffalo.

"It was starvation there, too. Mom sent us money and helped us buy a van. She believed in what I was doing. Barbara worked while I sang. I finally started bringing home about $100 a week. So did she. We did OK."

The Keystones started getting better acquainted with The Oak Ridge Boys when they booked the Oaks on several concert dates. William Lee Golden and Duane Allen already were in place in the group.

Richard had turned down an earlier offer to join the Imperials when the telephone call came from one of his heroes, J. D. Sumner, asking him to join the Stamps Quartet.

"We were struggling," Joe says. "Richard had three kids to feed. He just couldn't say no.

"We auditioned several bass singers, but we couldn't find one who sang as low as Richard. So we started performing as a trio, and we changed our style. We got successful imitating The Oak Ridge Boys. They were innovative, grew their hair long, wore neat outfits, and had a drummer. They were playing gospel music with a rock approach. I loved it.

"I hired a drummer and bass player. I started building the Keystones around the Oaks' image and music. Young people loved us. We used to call the Keystones an Oak Ridge Boys farm club."

The circle was drawing closer. The Keystones were booking the Oaks into the North and Northeast, while the Oaks booked the Keystones into large gospel festivals in the South.

When Richard and the Stamps weren't working with Elvis, the Stamps and The Oak Ridge Boys often worked concerts together. Richard and the Oaks were getting close, too.

"I was promoting dates with the Oaks in the Northeast and Canada and got to be good friends with them. William Lee was helping book us on some festivals, and Duane was starting his own record company and recording studio. The Keystones started making records for Superior, and Duane was our producer. We still didn't have a lot of money, but we had the support of my favorite people—The Oak Ridge Boys."

The Keystone Quartet kept at the business of singing. The group recorded several albums with Duane's record company.

"Duane Allen is one of the most powerful men I've ever known. When he's down, he can bring everyone down farther than the Atlantic Ocean. At the same time, no one else can lift you up with a kind word better than Duane. I'd get down and he gave me fuel for my fire for six months in those days."

In 1972, Richard left the Stamps to join the Oaks. A year later, Joe would complete the lineup we know as today's Oak Ridge Boys. Although he admired the Oaks and was pleased to get to work with Richard again, the decision wasn't an easy one for Joe.

"I knew the Keystones would not be my final place, and I knew that going with the Oaks would fulfill something I wanted for a long time. I knew the Oaks had the potential to be anything they wanted to be, and I wanted to be part of it.

"But I had my loyalties, and I was scared to death."

The worry came from the sound of what Joe calls "the big-time tenors" in gospel music.

"They could sing high and clean. I never sang like that. My voice always sounded different. It still does. Over the years, I realize that has been good. What I don't have in singing talent and sound I make up for by giving it everything I've got. I made up my mind right then that some tenor can come out and sing real pretty, but he had better have on his energy britches when I come on stage. I kick it with feeling, emotion, and energy. That is my biggest single blessing."

Joe was elated at joining the Oaks. But when he made that decision, he says, he and Barbara began to have problems. There was, however, another consideration. Barbara was pregnant.

"It was time to make the move. We loaded up everything we had and drove to Nashville in October 1973. Our daughter, Jennifer, was born that following March. She is the greatest thing that has happened to my life. I love her very much."

However, the die was cast, and Joe and Barbara would divorce several years later.

"My divorce was partly caused by my career. Barbara is a wonderful person. She still is. I don't have a bad word to say about her. She's a good woman who, for the most part, wished I had been an accountant, a youth director at church, and had come home every night.

"She is simple and laid-back, the exact opposite of me. I drove her nuts. Our early years together were very good. We probably would have divorced years earlier if we had not had Jennifer. She was the glue that held us together. Barbara moved back to Pennsylvania. I think she's relieved and glad to be away from the music industry."

Adding to the marital strain was what Joe described as "my self-destruct period."

"A lot of guys go through that in their twenties," he says. "I was kind of messed up myself. Barbara had a hard time handling it. Eventually, we kind of grew apart. It was easy to grow apart because we were so different."

Part of the problem, Joe says, was caused by pressure—the pressure of leaving one hand-to-mouth existence for another, more controversial one.

"The Oaks were progressive and innovative. We had to branch out, but traditional gospel fans rebelled against us. Groups went back to piano and preaching. We were a gospel group, but we were entertainers."

The years of 1975 and 1976 were particularly tough years, Joe says.

Enter Johnny Cash, Jim Halsey, and "Y'all Come Back Saloon." The Oaks become a hot country music act, and the financial worries were behind him. But troubles of another kind emerged.

"I think the road might have been part of my problem, too," Joe says. "I was a crazy son of a gun. I've never been able to do anything in moderation. I had a lot of energy channeled in different directions that could have come back self-destructive on me."

Joe says he was having problems with pills and liquor.

"It was a little of a lot of things—drugs, liquor, not taking care of myself. I was having problems with uppers and downers. I tried a few other things here and there. I drank too much. Sometimes, I would take a downer and then drink. I could have killed myself a few times.

"The pills were really getting to me. I was taking ups to get up onstage, downs to get down off the stage. I finally realized I owed the fans, my family, my partners, myself much more than that.

"That's when that little voice came back to me again. It talked to me, just as it did when I was lying in the back seat of that car after the gang fight when I was fourteen. It said, 'Straighten up. Life's too important. You've come too far to make a mess of yourself.' I never had to go to rehabilitation people. I just said 'OK. Knock this off.' "

During his "crazy" period, Joe found other temptations hard to resist.

"I loved women. They are there; they are pretty. For a long time, I didn't handle it too well."

Joe conquered his problems with a helping hand

from Duane Allen and the woman he calls the love of his life.

"I met Mary at a concert. She was with her sisters and mother. Her sister Vicki wanted autographs, so they all came backstage. We hit it off quite well. Mary and I went out for coffee after the show. She has turned my life around. Mary is my dream girl. She is everything I ever wanted in a woman. She has helped me straighten out a lot of parts in my life that were mixed up. She was the healing balm for my life.

"I just know that, since I met Mary, it hasn't been hard for me to overcome any temptations that may be out there. Our relationship is the best a couple could possibly have, and I will not do one little thing to mess it up. You can get in trouble if you want to. Anyone can. If you don't make yourself available, you can't get in trouble. After a show, I go to my room and play music, work on some songs, and play with my portable keyboard. Maybe I'll watch some sports on TV. By the same token, if you go to a bar and slug down a few drinks and sit down with a bunch of chicks that came to the show, you can get yourself in trouble. Well, I don't do that. I expect the same loyalty from Mary. Double standards don't wash with me.

"As I get older, I function better with positive things happening. If negative things come into my life, I have to get rid of them right then . . . get it on the table, wash it away, and move forward."

Mary and Joe have been married for four years. His daughter, Jennifer, spends part of the year with her father. Also sharing the home is Mary's daughter, Sabrina.

"I used to not be able to sleep at night. Funny, but for the past five years I sleep like a baby. I haven't touched any pills, and I don't drink anymore. I have a good bottle of wine with dinner once in a while, but that's it. Hard liquor makes me ill. It really does."

There are many positive elements enriching Joe Bonsall's life these days.

"I've grown up a lot; I've matured. My family life is together. My mom and dad are doing all right. My daughter is growing up into a wonderful young woman. Mary and I have a good relationship. So many positive things."

His career is more fulfilling than ever.

"Every year I get to do this, I feel I'm a fortunate man. The Oaks have been a big act for a long time now. People still pay their hard-earned money to see us. I take that as such a high compliment. I love this business more than I ever have.

"My routine these days is very simple. I like being home. But I know it's time to go back on the road, so I go. I do my job the best I can so I can get back home again and get ready for the next time to go out.

"I'm in a town that night for the show. My focus is on that show; everything I do is for that show. Then I do it. That's the reward time. I go back to my room, unwind, relax, get out my keyboard, work on a song, call home, call my mom or my sister, call Jennifer. I listen to music or watch TV. Then it's time to get on the bus and do it over again."

That routine is the "easy stuff," Joe says.

"Being away is the greatest price of a career in the music business. Not getting to see your mom and dad as often as you need to see them, being away from your wife at times you should be together, being away from your children at times when they are growing up. That is the price."

The rewards, however, have been great.

"I never thought much about financial success, but it does make things easier, being able to pay the bills and live comfortably. I also can do a lot more for my folks."

Along with those rewards have come the pressure.

"The pressure comes with the business decisions.

We have built such an intricate business over the years. We are realigning what we are doing. We are changing our way of doing things. We want to take some weight off our shoulders so we can concentrate on making better records, giving even better performances."

Joe's creative passion is songwriting. Oaks fans already have had a taste of his work. He wrote "It's Christmas Time Again" and "First Christmas Day" for the group's 1986 Christmas album.

"I'm no Kristofferson, but I'm pretty proud of some of my songs. I'm learning to put my feelings on paper."

Joe and his wife have started a music publishing company, B's in the Trees. It is affiliated with ASCAP.

"If all the work and effort I put into writing songs does pay off, I would like to have total control of it. I'm looking to the future, for the years I can't be on the road. It also might be a big thing for our daughters someday."

Along with his writing, Joe says he would "love" to do a solo album of his own songs. How would it sound?

"There is a harder edge to me than a lot of what the Oaks do. I would like to do a solo album and stretch myself musically."

However, that doesn't mean Joe is interested in leaving the group.

"That just won't happen, unless the Oaks kick me out. The secret of staying together, whether you are talking about your partners or your relationships, is communication. You also have to be careful about outside forces. Sometimes, you can listen to the wrong people who aren't in your shoes. They don't know what they are talking about. And that can hurt you. If I do a solo project, I won't have anyone from the outside pry me from the Oaks.

"I love all three of my partners. We are four very

different personalities and musically different. In this group, we have a high-fashion look, a mountain man, a guy who would rather be on his tractor, and me. I'm just a big ol' city boy, a grown-up street kid. Somehow, we've managed to pull it all together. That's our magic."

When it comes to picking songs to sing with the Oaks, Joe admits he has a preference for songs "that romp and stomp."

"It was our producer Ron Chancey's idea for me to sing the ballad, 'I Guess It Never Hurts to Hurt Sometime.' That was a real departure for me."

When he needs a departure from work and singing, Joe usually turns to music and sports for relaxation and stimulation.

"I play tennis, water-ski, and I work out. I love my music; I like listening to Bruce Springsteen and Journey. I enjoy movies. When I was a kid, I thought having a theater in my house like the rich people in Hollywood did would be pretty neat. I wanted to see first-run movies at home. I loved *West Side Story*. I used to dream of being Tony, running through the streets singing 'Maria.' Thanks to the videocassette recorder, we can sit at home and rent first-run movies. I love movies, sports, and rock and roll."

Joe is, as you might expect, a die-hard Philadelphia sports fan—baseball's Phillies, basketball's 76ers, and football's Eagles. "When any of my teams play, I almost get suited up. I've got to put on a jersey or something."

He also loves practical jokes—both giving and receiving. When there is any tomfoolery afoot during the Oaks' tours, you can bet Joe is usually right in the middle of it.

"I get a kick out of a good laugh. I get picked on and teased all the time. I'm a real instigator of practical jokes. Duane Allen is pretty good at that, too. Although he doesn't participate in the stunts, Richard has a really funny sense of humor. When he decides to come out with something, it is unique and really funny.

"Some of the best times we've had is when we are all four up at the front of the bus swapping Oak Ridge Boys stories. That is really fun." Those cherished moments shared with his partners underscores a basic truth about Joe Bonsall: being an Oak Ridge Boy is his life's dream come true.

"The real reward of all this to me is that I'm living my dreams. I used to get in my room and play records by Elvis Presley and the gospel groups on the record player and sing in front of the mirror. I used to dream about that nice-looking girl that I got to look after and fight for. I have that beautiful woman in my life. I've had a microphone in my hand since I was sixteen. Only today, I don't have to sing in front of a mirror.

"I don't take our success or our fans lightly. I'm doing what I want to do for a living. There are a lot of talented people out there. I'm very lucky, and I'm very grateful."

Joe Bonsall still hears his little voice every now and then.

"It still speaks to me. 'Keep working hard. More amazing things will happen.' And I believe that voice. It's never been wrong yet."

We had a variety show, but it never did go. Back then, gospel is what people wanted, and that's what we tried to give them. Now, these boys, I guess they crossed over. I always wanted a group that would do something like that, but they were afraid to. If you deviate from gospel in the South, they'd hang you.—Deacon Freeman, Oak Ridge Quartet baritone singer, 1946–49

We're just an old gospel quartet with a rock and roll band singing country music.—Joe Bonsall, Oak Ridge Boys tenor singer, 1972 to present

8
THE OAK RIDGE BOYS HAVE ARRIVED

In October of 1973, Joe Bonsall had to feel like the luckiest guy in gospel music. He had joined The Oak Ridge Boys only days after they had signed with Columbia Records, a move that promised bigger recording budgets, better distribution and promotion, and the wider audience the Oaks always knew they could reach.

George Richey, Tammy Wynette's husband, had produced an album's worth of material with Willie Wynn singing the tenor part, but that was no problem. Willie's voice stayed on the group sections, and Joe went into the studio and resang all of Willie's leads.

The Oaks were already, in Joe's opinion, the best act in gospel music. He had been invited in at the top, and it looked like they were going even higher. They had the Columbia deal, they were averaging more than $1,000 a show, and they had appearances scheduled on the "Mike Douglas Show" and "Hee Haw."

The Oak Ridge Boys were flying, all right. They were headed right into a nosedive.

The first sign of impending disaster came early in 1974, when they filled out tax returns for 1973. The Oak Ridge Boys had grossed $304,000, but the bottom line was just over $20,000. And it was red.

More signs came in the mail. During the first week of January, Bill Golden sent out a letter to gospel deejays that likened Columbia unto a "vehicle that can certainly take us (and the gospel) even further into the fields of new audiences. To those people still searching."

If music directors could not play their music, the letter continued, "we'll understand because the Oaks were born to sing. Not to fight."

The responses were of the good news/bad news variety. We would be happy to play your record, they said, if we *had* your record.

Like all the major record companies at that time, Columbia did not service all radio stations with records (although any station not serviced could buy records at wholesale prices). Furthermore, Columbia did not sign the Oaks to promote them as a gospel act, but rather to broaden their appeal to include a country audience. The Oaks did give Columbia a list of key gospel radio stations, but their long-range goals—which were the same as Columbia's—left some of the small gospel stations out in the cold.

The general manager of WACX in Austell, Georgia, spoke for many small radio stations when he first wished the Oaks the greatest success and then expressed his disappointment at their move to Columbia.

"We receive *NO* distribution of Columbia albums," he wrote. "Heartwarming has always given us excellent service and this will be missed insofar as your group is concerned. Columbia ignores the small station. . . . The Blackwoods, the Statesmen, Wendy

Bagwell, all formerly with RCA, have gone back to the gospel labels—doesn't this tell you something???"

In a fan club newsletter mailed on May 13, Bill assured Oaks fans that they had only changed record labels—not direction.

"It was done with the intent of being able to distribute our message to a more massive audience," he said. "We want everyone to learn about the excitement of being alive. To forget negative, backbiting attitudes. And to just learn the joys of their own inner happiness and peace."

Ten days later, Herman Harper, former Oaks bass singer and now their booking agent with Don Light Talent, sent a letter to The Oak Ridge Boys. Light's office was one block away from the Oaks'—literally within shouting distance—but the matter at hand was serious enough to warrant some formality. The two-sentence letter read: "It has become imperative that we get together and make some clear decisions concerning the direction of the Oaks' career. Please call me at your very earliest convenience to set up a meeting time and place."

As Harper later explained, "They were talking going country, and you know how talk goes—in the gospel business especially. We were getting a lot of questions from promoters."

Despite the ominous signs, 1974 looked good. It looked like The Oak Ridge Boys could, after all, sell gospel to country audiences. They appeared on the two top syndicated country TV shows, Porter Wagoner's and the Wilburn Brothers', three times on "Mike Douglas," and on a Canadian special produced by Sam Lovullo of "Hee Haw." They went to Sweden again, then to England, where they became the first gospel group to play the giant Wembley country music festival.

The term *gospel rebels* began to appear everywhere—even in one of their own publicity releases, which called the Oaks "rebels *with* a cause." They severed their affiliation with the International Gospel Song Festival, but it seemed they could do no wrong. The $1,000 dates of the previous year had grown to $1,250 and $1,500, and some went as high as $2,000.

The Oaks had no less a power than Johnny Cash in their camp. On April 17, 1972, at a time when Cash was at the peak of his influence, he had written a letter to the assistant to the president of the Las Vegas Hilton International, where he had just finished an engagement.

"I would like to point out a fantastic singing group to you—they are called The Oak Ridge Boys," Cash wrote. "I have nothing to do with their careers or their songs, other than the fact that I like them. . . .

"They are not a lounge act," Cash went on. "Where they should perform and where they would be fantastic is onstage at the International Hotel as an added attraction with a superstar." He also enclosed several Oaks albums and offered to send a video clip of their appearance on his TV special.

In August of 1974, they did play the Hilton as the "added attraction." The superstar was Johnny Cash. The pay for the seven days was $7,500 plus rooms and food.

At the end of August, they traveled to Saratoga Springs, New York, to participate in the American Song Festival, showcasing the winning song in the gospel category. There they met Larry Goldblat, former manager of the hit pop group Blood, Sweat and Tears.

"Out of that whole festival," Bill recalled, "he felt that The Oak Ridge Boys had a lot of potential. He said we needed personal management. He felt that with our potential as singers and musicians we should be in a different league of the entertainment business than what we were being pushed in."

They signed with Goldblat and canceled all their gospel bookings. Their cover version of Johnny Russell's country hit, "The Baptism of Jesse Taylor," was nominated for a Grammy as best gospel performance. And Columbia announced plans to release in early 1975 the first nongospel Oak Ridge Boys single, a love song written by former band member Greg Gordon called "Bringing It Back."

The first of 1975 came, and they won the Grammy. But Columbia did not release "Bringing It Back," and The Oak Ridge Boys still had not seen the first booking from Goldblat. With Bill having marital problems, Duane took over some of the booking, enlisting Richard's and Joe's help in contacting promoters in the Northeast.

It was not easy. Gospel promoters, as Herman Harper had warned, were indeed wary.

"The gospel people did not know where we were," Duane said, "and the country music people thought we were a big gospel group and didn't need the country dates. We were starving to death and nobody would believe us—except our banker.

"Our banker, Charlie Bryan, told me something that hit me harder than anything at that time. He said, 'Duane, I've never met anybody in my whole life in the music business that has a better feel and commonsense knowledge of the music industry than you.' Well, man, I got up on a pedestal. Then he said, 'But I believe you're the worst businessman I ever met in my life.'"

Bryan introduced Duane to Bob Bell, an accountant who informed the Oaks that their net worth was minus $114,000—the difference between their assets and their debts (*not* their operating losses for the year, as has been widely reported).

They signed a booking agreement with the giant William Morris agency for a short time, but still nothing happened. Eventually they found a savior in

Jim Halsey, who owned a booking and management agency based in Tulsa, Oklahoma. Halsey first saw the Oaks on a Columbia showcase during the annual deejay convention in Nashville in October of 1974. He was impressed, and he told them so. He later told them he thought they could be more successful with a more country style of music.

In the summer of 1975, Halsey booked Roy Clark and Mel Tillis on a show in Warwick, Rhode Island, and when Clark became ill, he called The Oak Ridge Boys to fill in. By August, he had them headlining for three weeks at the Landmark in Vegas. At Halsey's suggestion, they added three well-known country songs to the act: "Silver Wings," "Let Me Be There," and "Faded Love."

Their entrance on opening night was not encouraging. Comedian Pat Buttram, their opening act, was ill and on medication, and he introduced them as "The Oak Creek Boys." But the crowds were good and responsive.

"They were sensational," Halsey recalled, "but it was just enough money to eat." Halsey did not take his 10 percent booking fee, which would have amounted to $600, and the Oaks found themselves in the unusual situation of having a $500 surplus after the engagement. It was immediately spent on stage clothes.

"We were wearing wool suits—the only suits we had alike, the only good-looking suit we had that wasn't worn out," Duane said. "On the last half of the show, we dressed down to other clothes. It was so hot we couldn't stand it."

The new suits, made by Harvey Krantz, were of the same design with a different color for each singer. Although the Oaks jokingly called them "the doo-dah suits," they wore them for more than four hundred shows.

The problem with Columbia was not so easily

solved, however. "Bringing It Back" was never released as a single by the Oaks (later, Elvis Presley
and Brenda Lee would both have hits with it). Instead, "Rhythm Guitar," which they had sung at the
American Song Festival, was released. "Nobody
wants to play rhythm guitar behind Jesus," said the
song. Gospel radio's response was more like "Nobody
wants to play 'Rhythm Guitar,' period." (In 1979,
after the Oaks had become country stars on another
label, Columbia tried "Rhythm Guitar" again, on
country radio this time. It lasted one week on the
charts, peaking at #94.)

And there was another problem with Columbia. A
year earlier, radio stations couldn't get albums from
Columbia, and now the Oaks couldn't either. They
had none to sell at shows, which, according to a 1973
article in *Record World,* accounted for 20 percent of
their total album sales. Under the normal label/artist
arrangement, the Oaks were charged for those albums (at a better-than-wholesale discount), but the
charge was deducted from their royalties. That
worked fine at Heartwarming, where they sold two
hundred thousand albums a year, but at Columbia
their sales dropped to forty thousand, and they found
their account overdrawn. Having never had to pay up
front for albums before, they had not set aside any
money to do so. Consequently, when they set up the
record racks in the lobbies of their live shows, they
had only three-year-old Heartwarming albums to
offer for sale.

"We found ourselves getting lost in the shuffle
there," Bill recalled. "We went from being the top of
Heartwarming, one of the top acts on their label, to
Columbia with three hundred acts, where we became
about the three hundredth act down, the very bottom
of the label priorities. Although we cut some records
that we felt were good, at that time they didn't feel
like that was what they wanted to promote. Maybe

they didn't feel like there was a marketplace for them. It seemed like neither one of us knew the musical direction that the other one wanted to be in."

Through 1975, Halsey kept the Oaks alive by booking them on country dates with Johnny Cash, Roy Clark, Mel Tillis, and Jimmy Dean, while he tried to implement his master plan for the group. The plan, he explained: "Get them to broaden the music, get them on shows, get them seen, get them a record deal."

Broadening the music meant doing more country material.

"Getting them to change part of the show to country wasn't easy," Halsey recalled. Despite the slow but steady progress of Halsey's country bookings, some of the group members wanted to hang on to the security of the gospel audience until the country audience became established. And to that end, they felt it important to continue working the bigger gospel shows.

"I felt we could have hits with that top-of-the-fence music that talked about sky and birds and heaven and not necessarily about God, the church, and Jesus," Duane said.

Bill felt differently. The gospel backbiting he had hoped would be forgotten had only gotten worse. To be criticized as a country act was particularly rankling to him because, he said, "All the other groups in the business were *listening* to country music. That's what they would put on the radio. Even the Happy Goodman Family."

If the Goodmans were in fact listening to country radio in 1975, they would have been incensed to hear The Oak Ridge Boys singing behind Jimmy Buffett on a song called "My Head Hurts, My Feet Stink, and I Don't Love Jesus." Even though the song was a humorous account of a hangover—not a literal attack on religion—it was a clear sign that the Oaks would not last much longer in gospel music. And that was just fine with Bill Golden.

"I realized we had no future there," he said. "And if that was where our future was, then if we didn't get out, we might as well choose a different route.

"If that was what Christianity was all about, then I had totally the wrong concept of what it was supposed to represent. I thought it was the teachings of love and of fellowship and brotherhood rather than a religion of hate and jealousy and selfishness and greed. If some of the people had put melodies to the words that some of those people were saying and then tried to sell that, I'm afraid it would have been X-rated on some of the rock and roll stations today."

The Oaks still had many loyal fans, of course, but some of their fellow performers were now actively trying to run them out of business.

"One family group," Bill said, "really made campaign efforts to keep the promoters from booking you. They tried to boycott you through back-door, closet meetings with the promoters."

They were to a large degree successful. Gospel music at that time was controlled by five major promoters, Duane explained.

"The last year we worked solely singing gospel music, never singing one country song, out of those five promoters, where normally you'd receive 150 dates a year, out of those people we got three dates. There were three of them that gave us one date each."

The last of those three was in Roanoke, Virginia. It marked the end of 1975 and the end of The Oak Ridge Boys as gospel singers.

The atmosphere among the artists at the show was not friendly to begin with.

"The Kingsmen and the Florida Boys just about had a fight over who was going to use the sound set," Duane recalled. "Neither one would sing on the other's."

The Kingsmen took the stage, and they said something about The Oak Ridge Boys before they even started singing.

As Joe recalled it, "The exact words were, when they first came out and the lights were down, Jim Hammill from the stage said 'Wait! Turn these lights up. We're no nightclub act. They're coming out later.' "

It would get worse by the end of the Kingsmen's show. "They were really badmouthing us," Duane said. "And we're just about to come on, standing on the side of the stage in a coliseum with no backdrop. We're out in full view, our band already out onstage."

William Lee picks up the story. "They encouraged some of the Christians, when they left the stage and the rock and roll group comes onstage, they encouraged them to leave the building 'like they're doing.' "

Joe remembers a slightly less direct invitation to the audience. "I don't remember the exact words," he said. "but it was something like, 'If you're still in the building when they come out here, I know I won't be.' "

Eldridge Fox, leader of the Kingsmen, freely admits that his group made some remarks from the stage many times over about The Oak Ridge Boys, particularly about their musical direction. He said he felt the Oaks were "killing our profession." But he emphatically denies ever encouraging an audience to walk out. His exact words were, "That is a lie."

Whether or not the Kingsmen said it is of little importance compared to what happened next.

"We came on," Duane said, "and the first song we sang was 'Dr. God' [a song about trouble and confusion in religion], and the lyrics of that really apply to what happened in the next two minutes. Right in front of us was a congregation that had approximately two hundred members in it—one particular church. We started singing, and those people all stood to their feet, turned around, and stomped out.

"When that happened, I decided that I did not need that type of music anymore if that's what I had to deal with. I don't want to be a Christian if that's what a Christian is. They organized an event to try their best to embarrass and humiliate us. That's not Christlike. I decided that since they don't treat us Christlike, we might as well go to Vegas and sing out there where they treat us at least like decent men.

"And I found that no matter where you go, the God that I was singing about all my life up to that date, He's alive everywhere. Now you might not be singing about Him all the time. You ain't talking about Him all the time, either. And it finally got through my skull."

So it was good-bye, gospel; hello, Las Vegas.

"Everybody, after that concert, they *could not wait* to get out of there," Bill said, "to get out of the building, to get on the bus, and to head for Las Vegas and work with Roy Clark for two weeks. And after that two weeks, we were headed to the Soviet Union for three weeks."

With Roy Clark, The Oak Ridge Boys played eighteen shows in twenty-one days in the Soviet Union. In response to Russian censors, no one gave any religious testimony, and the word *Canaanland* in the song 'Where the Soul Never Dies' was asked to be changed to *Disneyland* by Soviet authorities. Otherwise, the Oaks performed their regular show. The word "Canaanland" was eventually performed as "that sweet land."

The tour was an unqualified success, any way you looked at it.

"It was like a graduation point," Jim Halsey said. "You are a worldwide attraction when you are accepted in the USSR."

It was also a success in terms of human relations.

"I saw firsthand how music can change people's

attitudes," Halsey said. "We did eighteen concerts in twenty-one days. I saw their attitudes toward Americans change. They were put in a state of harmony with the music."

Despite their new status as worldwide stars, The Oak Ridge Boys arrived home in Nashville with ever-growing financial problems. Bill, with a net income of zero, had nothing left to lose except his goals and visions for The Oak Ridge Boys, and he held on to them.

"I didn't think of quitting—not until my work was complete," he said. "Now I could, because I feel like now they don't think I was pipe dreaming about all those things—all those times I tried to say what we could do musically."

Duane, married with two young children, had plenty to lose, and he took action—too much action as it turned out—to keep the group together. Unable to meet payroll, he paid some members out of their withholding tax fund. He was unaware that it was illegal, but the Internal Revenue Service was quite aware and called him in.

With nowhere to turn for the $10,000 he owed, he went to Johnny Cash and offered to sell Cash the publishing companies.

"He leaned back in his chair," Duane recalled, "and he said, 'Duane, I don't want your publishing companies, because later on when you boys start hitting, you'll be sorry you sold to me. You need to keep them. But if you need $25,000, I'll loan it to you personally. Because I believe in you.'

"He shocked me so much when he said that. I realized that at that point that man had more confidence in The Oak Ridge Boys than I did. I sat there for a couple—it seemed like an hour but I guess it was five seconds. I stood up and went over and shook his hand, and I said, 'Johnny, thank you very much for the offer. If I need it, I will call you, but you've given me a whole lot more than an offer for a loan.' "

The next morning, Duane met with the IRS man and pulled an unorthodox maneuver. With no concrete evidence of future income, he took the agent on a tour through the Oaks' offices, showed him all the employees hard at work, and asked him if he could accept ten post-dated checks for $1,000 each, spread over ten months. The man agreed.

"That was, I think, the lowest part of my career," Duane said. But he and the Oaks were able to pull out of it, thanks once again to Johnny Cash.

"At that time, Johnny Cash asked me to produce an album for him. I've never been more depressed in my whole life. That album has never been released— probably because my production was not superb— but I think Johnny Cash knew I needed something. That gave me a life that kept me going through about a four-month period of depression. Johnny gave us that thing.

"Then he gave us dates. He booked us for a week in Vegas, paid us way too much, then gave us a 10 percent tip, like a tithe. He called us into a meeting up in his suite, got right in the middle of us, and said, 'Boys, you think it's rough right now, but there's magic in the four of you. I can feel that magic. I know that magic is there, and anybody who sees you knows that magic is there. Don't break up.'"

The Oak Ridge Boys had some self-confidence now, but they still weren't selling any records. They had been on Columbia almost three years, and they had yet to see their names on a country records chart.

In an attempt to regain their lost gospel market, they went into Duane's Superior Sound Studio and cut the album that was for all practical purposes their swan song—both to Columbia and to gospel music. It was called *Old Fashioned, Down Home, Hand Clappin', Foot Stompin', Southern Style, Gospel Quartet Music*, and it was a showcase of everything

The Oak Ridge Boys had done in gospel music.

For the first time since the Heartwarming days (and the last time, as it would turn out), the Oaks recorded with their band, giving listeners a true representation of what the live show was all about. The material ranged from an old-time quartet number to a gospel-rocker with lead vocal by Mark Ellerbee. There were country-arranged numbers— one written and sung by Johnny Cash, another featuring guest appearances by Charlie Daniels on guitar and Pete Drake on steel—and a gospel ballad each for Richard and Joe.

It was an album the Oaks could take pride in. It was everything they were at the time—versatile, spirited gospel singers. But it didn't sell any better than their other Columbia products.

Duane became so frustrated that he walked into the lobby of Columbia's Nashville offices and screamed, "Is there anybody in this whole building who can release me from my contract?"

Billy Sherrill, producer of Tammy Wynette and George Jones among many other hit artists, heard him. Sherrill promised to get the Oaks a producer and a hit single or release them. Dave Malloy, who later produced Eddie Rabbitt's hits, was enlisted, but after three songs, he left the project. One of those tracks, "Family Reunion," was released as a single, and it rose as high as #53 on the charts, peaking on June 26, 1976. But it was too little, too late.

By the early part of 1977, Billy Sherrill made good on his promise. He called the offices of CBS, Columbia's parent company, in New York to get the Oaks' release.

"We waited months," Duane recalled. "I had talked with Halsey, and I knew we had another label interested if we could get off of CBS. We were in New York City and had Sherrill on the phone. The CBS lawyer [in New York] said, 'The letter's in the mail.' Sherrill said, 'Read it.' They didn't have it, so he said, 'Type it.' I called the secretary, and she said, 'The release is in the mail.' I said, 'No, there's a guy walking in your door right now, and that guy is William Lee Golden. His name is on the contract. Give it to him.' I got in a cab and went to ABC. The button was pushed."

In the meantime, they were nominated for another Grammy Award, and they appeared on the awards show in February of 1977 as both performers and presenters. They won the 1976 award in the traditional gospel performance category for "Where the Soul Never Dies," the "Disneyland" song from the Russian tour.

Jim Halsey's bookings had kept the Oaks alive for two years, and in early 1977, they put their career in his hands, signing an exclusive booking and personal management agreement. Halsey was "twisting Jim Foglesong's arm," as Duane put it, at ABC/Dot Records. Out of courtesy to Halsey, Foglesong asked his head of a&r (artist and repertoire), producer Ron Chancey, to see the Oaks in Oklahoma City.

Chancey was reluctant.

"No one at the label was interested in them because they thought of the Oaks as a gospel act—as I did," he told *Billboard* in 1984. "What I saw onstage that night just knocked me *out*. I couldn't believe they weren't having hit records, so I came back and signed them."

By the end of May, they had finished a thoroughly country album. The enthusiasm they expressed to a *Tennessean* reporter came no doubt from several sources: the new album, the feeling that the burden of gospel music had been lifted, and the fact that, thanks to an advance from ABC, accountant Bob Bell was able to report that The Oak Ridge Boys' net worth was finally a positive figure. Among their comments:

Bill: "The album is just great. We're having more

fun now than we've had in our whole lives—everything is going strong. It's exciting when you're able to work in a variety of ways and keep yourself flexible. It keeps you from getting into a rut or bored. Your career is stimulated."

Richard: "The sound we've got on the album is definitely different. It doesn't have that gospel quartet sound that people are used to—it's definitely country-flavored."

Joe: "I just feel like we're being more honest now by expanding into other kinds of music. . . . When we sing gospel now, it's because we want to, as we do with other kinds of music—not because we have to."

Duane: "It's really a pleasure now to do gospel things for people who have been friends and fans for a long time, because it's not a chore, something we're expected to do exclusively. We don't want to be categorized as any one kind of group, whether it's gospel, country, or rock—and we do all of those. We just keep our minds open to doing good music of whatever kind and feel like our fans will want to come with us too."

In June, the title cut of the album *Y'all Come Back Saloon*, was released as a single. The Oaks and Chancey utilized one trick from gospel—the vocal shift of the melody near the end of the song, which switched the lead from Duane to Joe—and the song did contain the word *benediction*. But with the word *saloon* in the title, there was no doubt that the song and the artist were country.

As the album cover showed, they weren't sitting on the gospel/country fence any longer. They were sitting at a bar in a western saloon, dressed in cowboy duds, with six of the eight members sporting facial hair. There would be no going back to gospel now.

Also in the front cover shot (though not the back), the four singers were grouped together. Ever since they had had a band, the Oaks had always—in interviews as well as in publicity shots and album cov-

Photo by Alan Messer

Photo by Annie Leibovitz

Photo by Annie Leibovitz

Photo by Alan Messer

Richard and Joe backstage with Johnny Cash.

Courtesy of the Las Vegas News Bureau/MGM Grand

Lee Greenwood dealt blackjack in Vegas before signing
a recording contract. Here, the Oaks have him
outnumbered at the MGM Grand Hotel Casino, where
Greenwood opened for them in November 1983.

Photo by Wayne C. Kodey

During a December 1985 concert at the MGM Grand Hotel, T. G. Sheppard and Steve, Rudy, and Larry Gatlin came onstage dressed as Joe, Duane, William Lee, and Richard (respectively) with Mike Campbell (in black wig and dress) as Elvira.

Photo by Jon Mir

With Kenny Rogers.

Joe Bonsall when just a lad.

Joe and wife Mary dance in a scene from the 1985 music video of "Little Things."

At hometown, Philadelphia.

Cowboy Duane.

Duane Allen Day was declared in his hometown of Paris, Texas, on July 31, 1980.

Duane and Norah Lee Allen.

Richard Sterban, Minor League Baseball team owner.

In the recording studio.

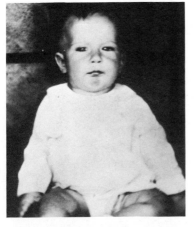

Wedding picture of William Lee and Luetta, with son Craig Golden.

The many faces of William Lee Golden: the '40s, the '60s, the very late '70s, and the '80s.

At the 50th All-Star Game, where they sang the
National Anthem, the Oaks met Johnny Bench.

On the set of "Good Morning America" with co-host Joan
Lunden.

The Oaks made a vocal appearance on Ray Charles's
Friendship album.

A 1986 appearance on "Hee Haw."

Copyright © 1984 by Scott Newton/Austin City Limits

Photo by Annie Leibovitz

The Oaks have been very active in children's causes, including work with the Boy Scouts and work against child abuse.

ers—projected themselves as an eight-man unit. Now for the first time, and forever after, The Oak Ridge Boys would be pictured as four singers with a backup band—a band that didn't play on the albums.

"Y'all Come Back Saloon" went to #3 on *Billboard*'s country charts, and the album eventually went gold (500,000 copies sold). The follow-up single, "You're the One," was released in November and went to #2.

As 1977 ended, The Oak Ridge Boys received two Grammy nominations, one in country for the "Y'all Come Back Saloon" single, the other in gospel for "Just a Little Talk with Jesus." They won in gospel. It was their fourth Grammy.

In February of 1978 (the month of the Grammy Awards presentation), the third single from *Y'all Come Back Saloon*, "I'll Be True to You," was released. It continued where the previous two left off and hit the #1 spot on *Billboard*'s country charts.

The Oak Ridge Boys never looked back in 1978. Their second album, *Room Service*, was released in May, and it, like all their albums to follow, went gold. The two singles from the album, "Cryin' Again" and "Come On In," both went to #3. They picked up another gold album, a present from pop star Paul Simon for singing backup on his hit single, "Slip Sliding Away."

Their live show reflected their new prosperity. *The Tennessean* reported they were now getting as much as $20,000 a night. They experimented with (and later added) lasers at the Tulsa International Music Festival. They returned to Roanoke, the site of their farewell to gospel music almost three years earlier, and according to a local review, they stole the show from headliner Mel Tillis. By the end of the year they were buying two more buses—one for the band, one for the crew. They were invited by Princess Caroline of Monaco to perform there on New Year's Day, 1979, to benefit the Year of the Child.

In the meantime, the Country Music Association

announced its nominations in the fall of 1978. In the vocal group category, the Oaks were up against the Statler Brothers, who had won for the previous five years. This year *should* be different, a cocky Duane told syndicated columnist Jack Hurst.

"I feel we're deserving, and I don't mean that egotistically," he said. "I think we're doing a lot more things than they are. They've not been on television, and we're on every time you turn the dial. And this year our records have edged out theirs. If you compare the careers, this year we deserve it."

They got it and then some. The singers were named Vocal Group of the Year, and the band was named Instrumental Group of the Year. The four industry trade magazines also jumped on the Oaks' bandwagon. The Oak Ridge Boys were named *Billboard*'s Number One Country Music Group of the Year, *Cash Box*'s Country Vocal Group of the Year, *Record World*'s Number One Vocal Group of the Year, and *Radio & Records*' Country Vocal Group of the Year.

Through it all, they continued to put more distance between themselves and the gospel crowd. A story on the Associated Press wire quoted Richard as saying, "Most of us go to the cooler after the show," a reference to the once-forbidden beer on the bus. And they recorded a song called "Easy," about a woman who's "easy to love," which was banned from radio in South Africa because of its subject matter.

The Oaks did not let up in 1979. They released a third album, *The Oak Ridge Boys Have Arrived*, and received a Grammy nomination for "Cryin' Again." They added wireless microphones, flash pots, and fog machines to their show. Their tour with Kenny Rogers and Dottie West was the biggest road show in the country at the time. "Leaving Louisiana," released near the end of the year, and "Trying to Love Two Women," released in early 1980, gave them their first back-to-back #1 records.

As Duane had said, they were everywhere on TV. In 1980 they hosted "The Midnight Special" and appeared on "Solid Gold," both pop music shows. They won an award as Best Country Group on the televised Juke Box Awards program. They performed an a capella version of the national anthem at Royals Stadium in Kansas City before an American League baseball playoff game. And they taped radio commercials for Dr. Pepper and Bell Telephone.

Press clippings—all of them positive—poured in from almost every major newspaper and mass market publication in the nation. They were as big as any act in country music and probably bigger than they themselves expected to be. But Bill, thinking two years ahead as usual, foresaw an even wider acceptance for The Oak Ridge Boys.

In May of 1979, he told *People* magazine, "Inevitably our music will cross all borders and labels. Someday we're going to run across something that everybody will like at the same time. When *that* happens, we'll have made it."

That happened in 1981, and its name was "Elvira."

Written in 1965 by Dallas Frazier, "Elvira" had been recorded by at least nine others, with Frazier having the only thing close to a hit. Ronnie Gant, a song plugger for Acuff-Rose publishing company, heard a bar band in Texas doing the song and thought it would fit the Oaks. He pulled the demo off the shelf at Acuff-Rose and played it for Chancey, who played it for the group.

"We knew when we heard it it was going to be a hit," Duane said. "We didn't know how big a hit because we had never had anything that big."

The Oaks added one little touch that made their version different from the previous ones. When they got to the "oom papa mau mau" part, Richard took over with a tone that would literally shake people off of their seats in concert halls.

The single shot to the top of the country charts and then crossed over, as Bill had predicted two years earlier, to the #1 spot on the pop charts. The album, *Fancy Free*, sold a million copies (platinum status), and "Elvira" went on to sell two million copies, earning a platinum award, a rare feat for a single in any field.

Duane took a look at the past—not the Oaks' past this time, but the history of popular music—and came away with his own vision of the Oaks' future.

"In studying the music business over the last fifty years," he explained, "I've found that every decade, there's been a major thing, a major force, starting with Rudy Vallee, going from Rudy Vallee to Frank Sinatra, going from Frank Sinatra to Elvis Presley, going from Elvis Presley to the Beatles in the sixties. But in the seventies there wasn't one. I kept thinking in the seventies that we might be that act. I thought when we got 'Elvira' that we might be that act."

It was not an unreasonable assumption. "I'm Settin' Fancy Free," the follow-up to "Elvira," was on its way to the top of the country charts as the Oaks went back into the studio to try to record another "Elvira."

They came close. They found a song that had been sent to them by Dan Tyler, a Nashville lawyer who had just switched careers and become a songwriter. Tyler's two-year-old son had been trying to sing "Bah Bah Black Sheep" and was stuttering on the *B*s. Tyler and his wife Adele along with songwriter Wood Newton took the stutter and put it in front of a girl's name. Richard sang the "B-B-B-B-," they all came in on the title, "Bobbie Sue," and the Oaks had their third straight #1 single.

Throughout The Oak Ridge Boys' thirty-five-year history, however, their greatest successes were always closely followed by disaster. The early eighties were no different.

The signs were hard to see at first. The only

outward sign was the change in Bill Golden. Since the mid-1970s, he had been William Lee Golden, not Bill Golden. The Oaks, wondering what was going on, avoided any problems with the name change by just calling him "Golden" (as they still do today).

He had worn a very close-cropped beard for a few years, but now his beard as well as his hair grew longer with every publicity picture. And his hair had suddenly become much grayer, as he had quit dying it.

Something was happening, not only to William Lee but to the other three Oaks as well. With their new prosperity, they began pursuing outside interests. In 1978, Richard invested in the Nashville Sounds minor league baseball team. Joe, too, had baseball on his mind, and in 1981 he fantasized in a story for *Country Music* magazine about himself in the uniform of his hometown Philadelphia Phillies. Duane collected classic cars, raised dogs and cattle, and drove tractors around his land, among other diversions.

William Lee's interests, however, were in direct conflict—at least they seemed to his partners to be—with the interests of The Oak Ridge Boys. He let his hair and his beard and his fingernails grow long. His actions as well as his dress reflected his interest in the more primitive, closer-to-nature lifestyle of the American Indian or the mountain man.

"I have to be true to myself," he would explain to the *Globe* a few years later. "I have to find out who William Lee Golden is. Every hair has its own length, just as each person has his or her own growth potential."

He became the exact opposite of the well-groomed, sharp-dressed example he had set for all the Oaks, and the change had both private and public ramifications. Privately, in the cramped quarters of a tour bus, his animal skin clothing sometimes emitted an overpowering aroma. Publicly, the other Oaks were afraid that the rough, unkempt look would hurt the group's image.

William Lee was not worried at all, especially after the success of "Elvira" in the pop market. He had been going to rock and roll shows since they began. He knew that the way he looked or dressed didn't matter to rock fans because they were more interested in the honesty and truth of the music.

But it went beyond that. It seemed William Lee was separating himself and promoting himself as an entity apart from The Oak Ridge Boys. In October of 1981, he—not the group—staged an outdoor music festival, the Harvest Jam, at his hometown of Brewton, Alabama. For the grand finale, William Lee gave a solo performance of his favorite song, the Beatles' "Long and Winding Road." He later went to Muscle Shoals, Alabama, and recorded the song, again solo.

In February of 1982, *The Tennessean* ran a story about the Oaks renting Nashville's 10,000-seat Municipal Auditorium as a rehearsal hall for three days to break in their new show and new stage equipment. The last part of the article reported William Lee's interest in some mountain man organizations. The photo that ran with the story, however, was *not* of the Oaks at the auditorium, but a new poster William Lee had commissioned. It pictured him in fringed buckskin, unshaven and unshorn for a year, riding a horse bareback and holding on to its mane with one hand.

To the general public, all was well. "Bobbie Sue" had a long run on the charts. "So Fine," a remake of an old rhythm and blues tune, did not do as well, so MCA (which had bought out ABC by this time) released a country tune, "I Wish You Could Have Turned My Head," which reached #3 on the country charts.

Concert crowds were getting ever more enthusiastic. As Richard told a reporter, "When I was touring with Elvis, those concerts were crazy and exciting, and it is starting to get like that for us now."

The Oaks underscored their commitment to charities, particularly the Stars for Children organization, by releasing "Thank God for Kids" from their 1982 *Oak Ridge Boys Christmas* album. It was a touching song, and William Lee, who sang the lead, made it even more so on December 19 when he started tagging it with ". . . and grandkids, too," a reference to his newly born grandson.

They opened the new year with another smash single, "American Made," which went to #1. But on April 4, 1983, during the height of "American Made," *People* magazine published a devastating article.

A photo caption set the scene: "In style and song, the Oaks . . . were in harmony until Golden changed his tune." After a laudatory opening paragraph, the writer got down to the dirt.

The disagreements between William Lee and the rest of the group were described as an "undeclared cold war." William Lee and Duane did not speak for close to a year. A lawyer drew up a "letter of reprimand" from Duane, Richard, and Joe, which William Lee took as a personal attack.

Part of the problem, according to Duane, *was* personal.

"If Golden's personal tastes are stronger than his commitment to his job," he said in the article, "then he can dress or look however he wants—but The Oak Ridge Boys won't go on." But the bigger part was professional—William Lee's solo leanings.

The article did not so much rock the boat as embarrass the group. As the headline said, "After Months on the Warpath the Battling Oak Ridge Boys Pass the Peace Pipe." The silence had been broken and the problems aired (if not completely solved) months before the story's publication, and the Oaks followed the *People* controversy with another #1 single, a rousing, party-flavored, modern doo-wop tune called "Love Song."

The "Golden problem" was really only a communication problem, Joe explained. "He's sometimes the hardest man in the world to communicate with. I talk, I communicate, I'm loud. He's quiet. . . . Golden doesn't know how to come to you and say, 'Hey, guys, I've got some things in my head I'd kind of like to do. I'd like to get back into nature, maybe grow my hair and beard real long. I know it's going to look strange for a while, but I think everyone's going to get used to it.' Wouldn't that have been wonderful?"

But it didn't happen that way.

"Communication goes downhill," Joe continued. "We're all wondering, What in the heck is Golden doing now? Duane, who is very emotional, can overreact easily and get upset, especially when he thinks something is hurting the group."

The controversy, Joe maintains, was blown out of proportion.

"The big thing is that we *haven't* had many fights. It was big news just because we had one. It was a family spat. So what? A couple of guys had words. They got mad at each other. One goes into seclusion [Duane]; the other goes off and gets freaky and weird. They didn't talk for a few months. What the hell? People do that all the time. All you've got to do is get through it."

"Music is the great healer," said William Lee, and The Oak Ridge Boys followed their crisis with some of their best music, including "Ozark Mountain Jubilee" in 1983, "Everyday" and "Make My Life with You" (both #1) in 1984, and "Come On In" in 1985.

The personality differences remain, but Joe looks at that as an asset now rather than a problem. It is, he feels, the key to the past and future success of The Oak Ridge Boys.

"What's made us is the fact that we are so different," he said. "If we had all been alike and liked the same things, I think we would have been boring. We have different likes and dislikes but somehow we pulled it all together.

"Therein lies the magic of The Oak Ridge Boys."

It blows me away how the fans stay with us. That's humbling to the ground to me. —Duane Allen

I think it's neat that we get to do what we do. —Joe Bonsall

9
TOUCH A HAND, MAKE A FRIEND

It is a clear, sunny, and humid summer day in Atlantic City. The marquee at Harrah's Marina hotel and casino proclaims what many fans of The Oak Ridge Boys have known for weeks. The Oaks are about to open a three-night stand at the seaside resort.

Extended engagements such as this are welcomed by the group, the band, and the crew. It gives everyone a break from a string of one-night stands. For the road crew in particular, it is a welcome opportunity to catch up on sleep and, for a change, enjoy some time on the beach and other activities.

In situations like these, members of the Oaks' families often join them. Since Atlantic City is so close to home for Richard Sterban and Joe Bonsall, Richard's mother and Joe's parents and sister will be in the audience all three nights for each of the six shows.

Two semi-truck trailers loaded with equipment

already have arrived, and the crew is hard at work setting up the stage for the weekend's work.

When the Oaks hit the road, a veritable fleet of vehicles makes up the Oaks' convoy. In addition to the equipment trucks, there is a truck for concessions such as T-shirts, jackets, and tour programs. There also are four buses: Chocolate carries the Oaks, Chocolate Chip ferries the Oaks' band, Chocolate Shake is the crew's bus, and a fourth, unnamed bus carries additional crew.

It is quite a production getting the Oaks on the road and keeping them there. It is also an expensive one.

"It costs about $15,000 a day to keep us going," says Jon Mir, the Oaks' production manager. "That's including things such as salaries, hotels, food, fuel, busing and trucking expenses."

In a normal concert situation, the equipment and crew usually arrive around 9:00 A.M. after an all-night drive to begin setting up the stage and lighting for that night's show. The Oaks' bus usually arrives around 10:00 A.M., and road manager Raymond Hicks gets the men checked into the hotel. There they will catch up on their rest, perhaps do some interviews, or take advantage of the hotel's recreational facilities.

If there is business to be conducted, the four might meet in one of the men's rooms. Down in the showroom, Hicks is checking on last-minute details with Harrah's entertainment director Blake Cumbers and entertainment manager Bruce Rowe. By the time 4:00 or 5:00 P.M. rolls around, the Oaks and the band arrive at the concert hall for soundcheck. Then, maybe there's time for dinner or a light snack before getting ready for the night's show.

While all this is going on, back in Nashville the Oaks' office is a flurry of activity. The staff has been setting up press interviews, making arrangements with hotels for the Oaks, the band, and the crew, and coordinating personal and professional schedules for weeks in advance and making last-minute adjustments. It is their job to make the tour run as smoothly and hassle-free as possible.

The Oaks have had a few days off prior to the Atlantic City engagement. Richard and Joe have been in Philadelphia visiting friends and family and trying to catch the Phillies at a home game.

William Lee Golden and Duane Allen have spent the days at home with their families. The day of the show, they and road manager Raymond Hicks board an airplane in Nashville for the flight to Philadelphia. The Oaks' buses and crew already are on the way.

When Duane, William Lee, and Raymond arrive at the Philadelphia airport, Chocolate is waiting for them. Driver Harley Pinkerman and personal aide Charley Daunis greet the men with a smile and a joke, and the one-hour drive north to Atlantic City gets under way.

When the bus pulls into the seaside hotel in the early afternoon, fans already have gathered outside to greet the Oaks. Typical of many, sisters Anne and Carol Pate have been waiting several hours.

When William Lee and Duane emerge from the bus, they walk over to say hello. Both men recognize the two and many of the others who have been waiting for their arrival. The greetings are warm, like a reunion of old friends.

Carol and Anne have driven from their North Carolina home to see the Oaks and will attend all six performances. It is an inspiring display of loyalty that is typical of many of the Oaks' fans.

The glamor of Atlantic City, the cross-country tours, the luxurious touring buses, and the gold and platinum records represent quite a contrast to the Oak Ridge Boys of 1966. When Duane Allen joined in

May of that year, he bought a one-fifth share of the group for $1,500 and a one-sixth share of their Silverline publishing company, which at that time contained exactly four songs, for $100. From a total value of just over $8,000 then, the Oaks' organization has risen in worth to tens of millions of dollars today.

From the first part-time employee, Ruby Moore, hired in the late sixties, the number of people on the payroll has grown to more than 80. With their families included, Duane estimates the Oaks feed about 350 people.

Ultimately, though, it is the fans of The Oak Ridge Boys who feed the organization. It is the fans who have bought more than ten million Oak Ridge Boys concert tickets, more than ten million Oak Ridge Boys records, and a million Oak Ridge Boys T-shirts, caps, and jackets in the last decade.

One of the most appreciative of fan support is Joe Bonsall, who might not have survived his early years with the Keystone Quartet had it not been for the generosity of the fans.

"There were a heck of a lot of people out there who took good care of us through the bad years," he said. "We stayed at people's houses a lot of nights, lived with people a couple of days in towns. People would cook for us and make meals. Some old preacher's wife, wonderful as could be, would do our laundry and stuff and get us on the bus."

Duane always looked forward to playing dates in North Carolina during the Oaks' gospel days.

"The fans brought us the best fried chicken, country ham, and biscuits in the world," he said.

Not all gospel fans were Oak Ridge Boys fans, however, and there was a dark side to those years that the Oaks are now glad to have behind them.

"Right now I never ever hardly at all get a bad letter," Joe said. "In gospel days, half the mail you got was criticism—'Your hair's too long, your moustache, you'll never go to heaven with a moustache. You guys are too loud, the clothes you're wearing ain't right, your hair's not right, and your attitude's not right. Get your heart right with God if you want to sing gospel music.'

"Now every letter we get is like, 'Yay, The Oak Ridge Boys. We love you guys. We love your music.' We get hundreds and hundreds of Christmas cards, even birthday cards, and they're all from these people that just love the group, love the singing, love the music, and love the feeling they get when they come to hear us sing."

Oak Ridge Boys fans are hard to miss. They are literally everywhere. Their fan club membership numbers seven thousand (it swelled to ten thousand just after "Elvira"). During Fan Fair, up to three thousand of them come to Hendersonville for the annual fan club open house. They write twenty-five to fifty letters a day to the Oaks. There is a steady flow of fans in tour buses and private cars to the Oaks' offices and even to their homes.

Ever since the gospel days, fans have formed caravans behind the Oaks' bus.

"A woman and her daughter followed the bus all summer long," Duane said. "One time I asked her what her husband thought. 'Aren't you married?' 'Yeah.' 'What does your husband do?' 'He drives a truck.' 'Well, what does he think about you following us around like this with your daughter?' 'He follows Crystal Gayle.'

"They're nice people. It's weird, because I didn't think they would be. Sometimes you kind of miss seeing them out there. If all at once they're gone, you wonder if they're OK."

One of the most memorable fans actually stopped the show at an Oaks concert in Toronto. It was an outdoor, festival-type arrangement on a muddy field.

"A big old fat girl came running to the front of the

stage, and she had on a halter top," Joe recalled. "Boom! She fell in a huge mud puddle right in front of the stage. She had humongous breasts—I mean really big—and the funny thing was watching her trying to get out of the mud, half-drunk, and trying to stuff her breasts back into the blue halter top. She's pushing one in this way, and then the other one fell out this way.

"We were singing 'Come On In,' and it stopped us totally down. It was a big festival—thousands of people way to the back—and those people way back there probably didn't know what was going on, except that our song was falling apart. We quit singing, quit playing. We were laughing our butts off."

One of the highlights of any year for Oak Ridge Boys fans is the annual Oaks' open house held as part of the annual Fan Fair weekend in Nashville. The party includes a concert by the Oaks, or, in alternating years, an event such as a celebrity softball game. The fans also enjoy a picnic meal and gifts. Many of the twenty-five hundred to three thousand in attendance get an autograph, too. At the first one, the Oaks spent seven hours in a torrential downpour signing autographs for the more than three thousand fans in attendance.

"Going to Fan Fair is really a highlight for us," Duane said. "We try to do all of the fan-related events. It's very high-energy for us. We're not super people, but we try to be. We've got a super group of people out there that like us."

If the Oaks bend over backward to please their fans, it is because they know exactly what it is like to be a fan of the Oaks. William Lee, Duane, Richard, and Joe were huge fans of the Oak Ridge Boys before they became members.

William Lee remembers seeing the Oaks at an all-night gospel singing.

"When the Oaks performed, they woke the crowd

up and everybody paid attention. They could outsing any quartet and outperform them."

Joe was such an Oak Ridge Boys fan that he modeled his group The Keystones after his idols.

"The Oaks were rebellious, and yet they had the good image, and they were innovative in their music," Joe said. "I really fell in love with the Oaks. I looked up to them."

Duane chartered a bus from Paris, Texas, to take fifty people to see the Oaks in Fort Worth.

"I remember it well," Duane said. "Golden had black hair and a blue suit. I met him in the hall. I didn't talk to him, but I saw him. He went over good. I went to all three shows that night."

Away from the concert hall, the Oaks remember a time when Oak Ridge Boys fans staved off a potential problem for them. The men were standing in line for tickets to a series of Bruce Springsteen shows at the Meadowlands in New Jersey. Duane remembers what happened:

"We didn't go to the back door. Maybe it was because we didn't like to take advantage of people. We were standing in line like everybody else, and there was a group of guys that stood right in front of us. They looked like they could have been a football team.

"We were probably two hundred yards from the building in a solid line six wide clumped in the middle. People started yelling out our name, breaking in line, and pulling at us. It was beginning to cause a problem. Without the Oaks saying a word, that group of guys surrounded us and wouldn't let anyone bother us. They were Springsteen fans, and they were our fans, too. When we became one of them, standing in line, they took care of us."

The audience sees very little of what it's like to be an Oak Ridge Boy—a couple of hours at the most, the time between arrival and departure from a concert.

That appears to be and *is* a fun, exciting, and occasionally frantic few hours for the Oaks and their crew, but it represents only a fraction of their lives. A much larger piece of the Oaks' time is spent in a much less appealing activity—riding the bus.

The bus is as comfortable as it can be, with plush seats, sound systems, TVs, VCRs, and even a satellite dish. But after thousands of shows and hundreds of thousands of miles on the road, the mind gets restless. Consequently, The Oak Ridge Boys have given their fair contribution of proof to the old maxim "An idle mind is the devil's workshop." The proof comes in the form of practical jokes.

The one that garnered the most publicity has never before been revealed to be a joke. In 1971, bus driver Darrell "Curly" Jones and publishing manager Aaron Brown brought the bus back to Nashville from the Northeast and immediately called up *The Tennessean*. They told reporter Jack Hurst (now a nationally syndicated country music writer) that they had been stopped in Washington, D.C., by a bunch of "hippie-looking" war protesters who thought the name Oak Ridge referred to nuclear plants. Violence was narrowly avoided when Curly passed out some albums. "This idea not only worked to grant us release from the protesters, but we were then praised for the gospel work we were doing," Aaron Brown said. *The Tennessean* ran the story, but that's all it was—a story Curly and Aaron had made up to kill the boredom of the long drive.

Most of the time, victims of practical jokes are other entertainers or the Oaks themselves.

As Glen Allred, former Oak and current member of the Florida Boys, put it, "We aggravated them, they aggravated us, they aggravated themselves."

Allred recalls the time the Florida Boys put a stink bomb on the Oaks' bus, just as the Oaks were departing on a thirty-six-hour drive to the West Coast. The

Oaks got their revenge at a memorial show for
Smitty Gatlin when they loosed a bucket of crickets
on the Florida Boys' bus. The crickets got into the
ventilation system and it took months to exterminate
the last chirp.

The Oaks got the idea of the crickets from the
Speer Family, who had done the same thing to the
Oaks. For revenge that time, Duane recalled, "We put
our 'I Love the Oaks' stickers all over the inside of
their bus and filled it with empty record boxes."

Willie Wynn, the tenor singer whom Joe Bonsall
replaced, was the butt of many practical jokes.
Former Oaks bass singer Noel Fox recalled hiding a
stray dog in Willie's closet on the bus and attaching a
"popper"—a fireworks item that pops when its string
is pulled—to the door. Willie, who was afraid of dogs
to begin with, pulled open the door and almost had a
heart attack. Fox had to wrestle a .44 away from him.

Willie also was afraid of ghosts.

"I was constantly scaring him," Duane said. "I've
almost gotten killed because he would always come at
me. Willie was not afraid of anything but his
shadow."

Willie's biggest scare came when the Oaks played a
show in West Virginia that was promoted by a fu-
neral home owner. Duane hid in a casket while the
owner gave the rest of the group a tour. He opened up
Duane's casket, and Duane rose up. Willie, standing
at the head of the casket, couldn't tell who it was, but
when he finally caught his breath and recognized
Duane, he attacked him and had to be physically
restrained.

"Little David" Smith, who was playing guitar with
the Oaks at the time, was only fourteen years old, and
the sight of Duane rising from the dead caused him to
faint.

"He turned white and fell completely over on his
back, like a domino," Duane recalled. "Later that

night on the bus, he came and sat down next to me. He was shaking, and he started crying. It took him two days to get over that."

The Statler Brothers, arch-rivals in the eyes of many fans, are among the Oaks' favorite victims.

"We've always done stuff to the Statlers," Joe said. "All last summer [1985] we worked a lot of fairs. Every night we played where the Statlers were coming in, I'd get onstage and say, 'Ladies and gentlemen, the Statlers are coming.' I asked how many were coming, and a bunch always raised their hands. I would say, 'Wait until half of their show and then yell, "Sing 'Elvira.' " They did. The Statlers hated it. After a while they started singing a little of 'Elvira' and telling the audience, 'We'll show you how it should have been sung to begin with.' Which is real funny, I think."

One night in Independence, Kansas, the Oaks were working with Mel Tillis. "We came out in sheets and spooked him," Duane said. "When I went back to the bus that night, my bed was piled with garbage. And on top, the mangiest dog you've ever seen. It was awful."

In Las Vegas once, the Oaks had been ragging Larry Gatlin and the Gatlin Brothers and T. G. Sheppard, who were on the same bill at a hotel down the strip from the Oaks. There had been no response to the "little gifts" the Oaks had been sending. On the last night, while the Oaks were doing "Elvira," Sheppard and the three Gatlins walked onstage dressed as the Oaks, complete with rented wig and beard for William Lee and a rented moustache for Joe. The audience roared its approval at the antics.

Duane remembers a time when the mother and daughter duet, the Judds, got in a practical joke of their own.

"It was our next to the last night of our tour with them. While Joe was talking about our working with them, Wynonna and Naomi came out onstage with two 'APPLAUSE' signs and stood behind him, then they disappeared. The audience went wild."

As you might expect, the Oaks got their revenge.

"The next night, the crew went to a used-clothing store and bought a bunch of women's clothes," Duane said, laughing. "Golden, Joe, me, our road manager Raymond Hicks, and some of the band went out onstage during their show while they were singing 'Girls Night Out.' Heels and all. Except me. I refused to wear the heels. But the audience loved it."

On the Oaks' bus, the main rule to remember is not to make any noise if you get up in the middle of the night.

"Duane Allen may hear you," Joe explained. "He gets in the bottom of your bunk and scrunches himself up as small as he can get, waiting for me to get back. When I get back in, he screeches at me. It scares the life out of me."

Duane's stunt unexpectedly backfired one night. Joe got up and Duane positioned himself in the bunk. But Joe stayed up for a while to talk to the bus driver. Duane, hiding in Joe's bunk, began to get cramps after ten minutes and finally just gave up and went back to bed.

"Can you believe it? I got him back and didn't even know it at the time," Bonsall said, laughing. "Duane told me about it the next day. He thought it was pretty funny."

There also is a serious side to being an Oak Ridge Boy. The Oaks feel they have a certain responsibility to give back something for all that they have received. Consequently, they donate a great deal of time and talent to charities, particularly those that help children. They did a series of TV ads for the Boy Scouts of America, for which their staff songwriters Jimbeau Hinson and Michael Foster wrote the jingles. They are the national spokespersons for the

National Committee for the Prevention of Child
Abuse. In 1978 they founded the Stars for Children
program, and in the next five years the annual Stars
for Children concert raised more than $500,000 for
the prevention of child abuse.

Their involvement with the Make a Wish Founda-
tion has been a particularly emotional experience.
"We have been the wish—which really blows me
away—of a lot of kids that were dying of some
catastrophic disease," Joe said. "It was their final
wish to go see The Oak Ridge Boys and meet them.

"There's a double thing there. First of all, it tears
your heart because you feel, my God, this child right
here that I'm talking to is going to die soon. There's
nothing more depressing than that. But at the same
time there's always an inspiration and a lift-up experience, too, because you find so many of these kids
have tremendous spirit.

"It makes you feel again how many different ways
you as a major musical entity touch people. Here's
some kid. I mean, this kid is ten and he ain't gonna
make eleven, but he wants to meet The Oak Ridge
Boys. That's not a small thing. That's a big thing.
That's a real big thing."

The biggest challenge is trying to figure out how this is going to end. . . . Jim Halsey told us he felt like he would see an Oak Ridge Boys ten years from now. I don't know what the future holds because I think The Oak Ridge Boys are in a new era right now.—Duane Allen

I'm doing what I wanted to do, enjoying it to the utmost, and I'm very successful. Few in life can make that statement. My job is my main hobby.— Richard Sterban

I feel really fortunate to be right here singing. I said that when I was twenty-seven, and I said it when I was seventeen, and I'm saying it at thirty-seven, and I hope to God I'm saying it when I'm ten years older.—Joe Bonsall

The Oak Ridge Boys can go on to an even higher level—if The Oak Ridge Boys want to. And if I'm not the one chosen to sing the baritone part, then I'll be out in the audience applauding.—William Lee Golden

10

THE BEST
IS YET TO COME

William Lee Golden, Duane Allen, Richard Sterban, and Joe Bonsall defeated history. They faced and overcame all the obstacles that had thwarted The Oak Ridge Boys since 1945—dissension within the group, factional wars in the gospel music industry, and, consequent to both those factors, financial ruin. They didn't just survive; they achieved a level of success that surpassed even their own greatest expectations.

For the first time in their history, The Oak Ridge Boys do not have to worry about their future. Although record sales and fan club membership—two signs of their popularity—have fallen off from the period just after "Elvira," that was to be expected after such a gigantic hit. Their fans still worship them and flock to see them in numbers any country entertainer would envy.

They have accomplished enough musically, they have made enough money, and they are old enough that they might be expected to coast along now for as long as the ride lasts. Considering the loyalty of country music fans, that could easily mean for as long as they can stand on a stage and squeeze a sound out of their vocal cords.

But that is probably the *least* likely scenario for the future of The Oak Ridge Boys.

Jim Halsey considers it part of his job to see that The Oak Ridge Boys continue to grow. He had a plan in the beginning, and he has one now.

"We'll continue what we're doing," he said, "updating the look, the sound of the show, and musically, too. In the next few years I'd like to expand them into Europe.

"In my estimation, there have been three ultimate achievements: Sinatra, the Beatles, and Elvis. The Oaks are there as far as I'm concerned. Now we need to do it worldwide. It's a matter of making it better, fine tuning."

The Oaks are taking steps to ensure that growth and to scale new artistic heights. In the fall of 1986, the Oaks started working with producer Jimmy Bowen, who heads MCA Records' Nashville operation. It will be Bowen's first time in the studio with a vocal group.

At a Nashville news conference, the Oaks and Bowen made it clear The Oak Ridge Boys are not about to hang it up.

Joe just enjoys being an Oak Ridge Boy too much to slow down.

"When you have a record playing on the radio, man, it's neat for me to think that some guy working on a car in Portland, Maine, is listening. I don't know why I never got over that kind of thing. I enjoyed it at the beginning. I enjoy it now. When the Oaks are on the radio, I turn it up and get a big charge out of hearing the song on the radio."

The new audiences every night renew Joe.

"One night you're at the Salt Palace, one night you're at the Kansas State Fair, and people are cheering for you, applauding, having a good time. And you touch them—you're moving them with music. Ah, it's great.

"It's a thrill to me to see a little old lady out there clapping hands, getting rocked out of her seat for a few minutes and having a ball. That thrills me to see old people in the audience having a high old time."

For Richard, being an Oak Ridge Boy and continuing to be one is a matter of pride.

"When I see our name—The Oak Ridge Boys—on a sign or marquee, I feel a sense of accomplishment," he said. "I'm very proud of that."

To Duane, The Oak Ridge Boys are a dream come true.

"This was my dream, to be an Oak Ridge Boy," he said. "And I'm still dreaming."

For William Lee, "Being an Oak Ridge Boy means you can grow to your full potential, reach for tomorrow today."

William Lee's solo album at first caused waves, and communication was not what it should have been among the group members, according to Joe, but by the time the album was released in the spring of 1986, Joe was saying, "I think solo projects will help The Oak Ridge Boys."

Joe not only supported William Lee's solo effort; he was also busy writing songs for one of his own.

"I'd love to do a record of Joe Bonsall music," he said. "I'd like to stretch musically." He had one reservation about it, though. "I don't want to cause any problems with the group. I'd want everything out front. I don't care to leave The Oak Ridge Boys and sing on my own, unless The Oak Ridge Boys kick me out."

Richard does not see himself as a solo album artist. While his voice can rattle the seat bottoms at a

concert hall and drive a female audience into a
frenzy, he doesn't feel that it would come off well over
the course of an entire album.

For Duane, the solo issue is much more complex.
Since he joined The Oak Ridge Boys in 1966, he has
been in many respects a soloist. His first album with
them was, after all, called *Duane Allen Out Front.* So
important was his presence in the group that all their
record contracts until the most recent one stipulated
that, if Duane left, the contract was void. (Now the
departure of any two members voids the contract.) If
there was one Oak Ridge Boy to do a solo album, the
obvious one was Duane. The opportunities and even
the encouragement from some people were there all
through the years, but Duane always refused out of
loyalty to the group.

"I always wanted to be a group man, not a soloist,"
he explained. "We *share* the applause, the good
things, and the hassles. It is a shared thing."

The opportunity is still there for Duane, but the
idea that a solo album by *any* member would take
away from The Oak Ridge Boys is still etched in his
mind. And furthermore, the group satisfies all his
artistic needs.

"The group is magic," he said. "We add up to a
bigger one than me alone. We can compensate for
each other's weaknesses this way. We've all had hits.
All four of us have sung lead on hits. We've all been
soloists within the group. I'm on every record, and
that's enough for me."

Despite Duane's and William Lee's differing opinions on the subject of solo albums, Duane's love for
The Oak Ridge Boys is shared by William Lee.

"I didn't start The Oak Ridge Boys, and I certainly
don't want to be the one to stop it," William Lee said.
"I think The Oak Ridge Boys have the potential to go
on a lot longer than any of us—if The Oak Ridge Boys
want to.

"And I think it's selfish of us—any of us—to think that it shouldn't. And it's egotistic and narrow-minded to think that," he continued. "Since it was going on a hell of long time—twenty years before William Lee Golden came along—it surely should go on twenty years after I'm gone from the group."

Due to the increasing diversion of the Oaks' outside interests, they decided to take a break from music in the spring of 1987 to pursue those interests. It will be their first extended vacation ever. It could signal the beginning of the end for the group, but it is more likely the mark of a new beginning. There is too much pride in The Oak Ridge Boys, and the group has been such a major part of their lives for so long that they have a hard time envisioning themselves as *former* Oaks.

Joe believes the stability of the personnel in the group is crucial to the future. They have been a unit now for fourteen years, and that is the one difference between the current Oaks and all the unsuccessful configurations over the years.

Richard sees himself singing for another ten years at least. If it all ended now, he might pursue his two primary goals outside of music—developing a fashion line and owning a major league baseball team.

Duane simply can't picture himself without The Oak Ridge Boys.

William Lee *is* able to think about The Oak Ridge Boys without himself. Ever the visionary, he sees a time when there may be an all-new Oak Ridge Boys.

"Progress must go forward," he said. "I don't want to hinder anyone or overstay my welcome or contribution. I'd want to be proud that we had carried the torch as far as we could carry it, that when it's time to pass it to a new runner—*singer*—they would carry it with the same enthusiasm we had."

Personally and professionally, Jim Halsey knows The Oak Ridge Boys better than anyone, and his vision of the future of The Oak Ridge Boys extends beyond the individuals who make up the group today.

"I think the *group* is the entity," Halsey said. "There were many people before these four. Like the Glenn Miller Orchestra, it's the music, the energy that made it continue. I can see an Oak Ridge Boys forty years from now.

"They haven't started yet, as far as reaching their full potential. The world's out there for the Oaks."

A ROLL CALL OF MEMBERS

Wally Fowler, Lead Singer

From Bartow County, near Rome, Georgia.
Founded the Oak Ridge Quartet, 1945. Sold the
group to Bob Weber in the early fifties. Oversaw
the formation of and suggested the name for the
"new" Oak Ridge Quartet in late 1956. Sold the
name to Smitty Gatlin in return for debts owed in
the early sixties. Still performing, based now in
Branson, Missouri.

The North Georgia Boys

Sang around Rome, Georgia, from 1936 to 1941. Were
(with Wally Fowler) the original Oak Ridge Quartet:

Curly Kinsey, Bass Singer and Guitarist

From near Summerville, Georgia. Member of the
Four Tones in early forties. Joined ORQ (Oak Ridge
Quartet) in late 1944. Left in 1948 to help start the

Louisiana Hayride, performing as Curly Kinsey and the Tennessee Ridge Runners (country) and the Four Deacons (gospel). Died in a car wreck in Summerville, Georgia, in 1963.

Johnny New, Tenor Singer and Standup Bassist

From Lindale, Georgia. Member of the Four Tones in early forties, disbanded in 1944. Member of Tobacco Tags in Raleigh, North Carolina. Joined ORQ in January 1945, left in 1949, rejoined in 1951, left in late 1951. Now a retired pastor of a Baptist church in Raleigh, North Carolina.

Lon "Deacon" Freeman, Baritone

From near Summerville, Georgia; founded Four Deacons gospel group in the Army. Joined ORQ in 1946; left in 1948 to help start the Louisiana Hayride, performing as a member of the Tennessee Ridge Runners (country) and the Four Deacons (gospel). Returned in fall of 1948, left in 1949 to form the Stone Mountain Quartet. Worked for Jewel Tea Company twenty-nine years. In the carpet business in Dalton, Georgia, since 1979.

Curly Blaylock, Bass

Replaced Curly Kinsey in the spring of 1948; left in 1949.

Neal Matthews, Baritone Singer and Electric Guitarist

Joined in 1948; left in 1949; after army duty, filled in on guitar with ORQ in early fifties. Joined the Jordanaires, who backed up Elvis Presley and developed the "Nashville number system" of music notation.

Instrumentalists with The Oak Ridge Quartet and the Georgia Clodhoppers, 1945-49:

Zeb Turner, electric guitar, 1945-46.

Joe Carrol, fiddle, joined in 1945.

Zeke Turner, guitar, replaced Zeb Turner, 1946.

Red Bennett, accordion.

Joey Ross, accordion, replaced Red Bennett.

Charles Bares, steel guitar, some appearances in late 1946.

Bill Stepp, piano.

Bill Byrd, guitar—left with Deacon Freeman and Curly Kinsey for the Louisiana Hayride in 1948; later played with Ernest Tubb; now drives a cab in Nashville.

Boyce Hawkins, piano—replaced Bill Stepp in 1949; became a successful announcer and weatherman on Nashville TV and radio.

Oak Ridge Quartet, 1949-56

Deacon Freeman, Johnny New, Neal Matthews, and Curly Blaylock left Wally Fowler in 1949 and relocated in Rome, Georgia, where they worked as the Stone Mountain Quartet.

The Calvary Quartet

From Statesville, North Carolina, became the Oak Ridge Quartet, making their debut on the Grand Ole Opry's Prince Albert show on November 26, 1949. They were:

Bob Weber, Bass

Left in 1956, less than two months before the Oak Ridge Quartet disbanded, to manage the Chuck Wagon Gang. Worked for the Downtowner hotel chain; now owns four hotels in Dallas, Texas.

Joe Allred, Tenor

Left in 1950 with throat problems and was replaced by Johnny New; rejoined in late 1951; left in 1953.

Bill Campbell, Guitarist

Left in 1951.

Johnny New, Tenor

Replaced Allred in 1950, left in 1951.

Pat Patterson, Baritone

Also sang lead in Fowler's absences; left when drafted in 1952.

Bobby Whitfield, Pianist

Joined in 1950; left when drafted in 1952; rejoined upon discharge in 1954.

Livy Freeman, Pianist

Replaced Bobby Whitfield in 1952; left when Whitfield returned from the Army.

Glen Allred, Baritone and Guitarist

Replaced Bill Campbell in 1951; let go in 1952; joined the Gospel Melody Quartet, now known as the Florida Boys.

Bob Prather, Baritone

Joined in 1952.

Walt Cornell, Baritone/Lead

Performed a double-talk comedy routine; replaced Bob Prather.

Carlos Cook, Baritone/Lead

Replaced Pat Patterson.

A. D. Soward, Bass

Filled in while Bob Weber took Army physical.

"Sister" Cat Freeman, Tenor

Replaced Joe Allred, 1953; filled in in 1957 after Hobart Evans left. Later sold Bibles; now retired and living on the family homestead in Fyffe, Alabama.

Calvin Newton, Lead

From West Frankford, Illinois. Replaced Walt Cornell; hired as baritone but switched parts with Carlos Cook after three weeks. After disbandment, tried nightclub singing for a short time, then formed the Sons of Song. Later a welder. Now living in La Fayette, Georgia.

Les Roberson, Baritone

Replaced Carlos Cook.

Ron Page, Bass

Replaced Bob Weber, fall of 1956.

In late 1956, the Oak Ridge Quartet disbanded.
Members of the group at that time were Calvin
Newton, Cat Freeman, Les Roberson, Ron Page,
and Bobby Whitfield.

The "New" Oak Ridge Quartet

Debuted at an all-night singing on New Year's Eve,
1956:

Smitty Gatlin, Lead

From Pulaski, Tennessee. Left in 1966 to be
minister of music at the First Baptist Church of
Dallas. Later formed the Smitty Gatlin Trio. Died
on March 20, 1972.

Ron Page, Baritone

From Decatur, Illinois, where he was a member of
the Gospel Four. Left ORQ in 1962 to host a daily
gospel TV show and sing with the Chuck Wagon
Gang. Ran unsuccessfully for U.S. House of
Representatives. Now hosts a daily gospel TV show
on a Murfreesboro, Tennessee, station.

Hobart Evans, Tenor

From Tuscaloosa, Alabama, where he was a
member of the Rainbow Quartet. Left ORQ in 1957
when a stove blew up in his face. Moved back to
Tuscaloosa.

Bill Smith, Bass

From Valdosta, Georgia. Lasted three weeks in
January, 1957.

Powell Hassell, Pianist

From Tuscaloosa, Alabama, where he was a
member of the Rainbow Quartet. Left ORQ in late
1957. Worked in a Memphis music store; district
manager for Harley-Davidson motorcycles, 1960–
68; owned the largest Harley-Davidson dealership
in Atlanta, 1968–76; originated the Formula 440
racing car and won the first Formula 440
championship at Road Atlanta raceway in 1969;
now lease manager for an Atlanta Honda
dealership.

Herman Harper, Bass

From Portland, Tennessee. Former member of the
Portlandaires and the Southlanders. Replaced Bill
Smith, early 1957; left in 1968 to go into
partnership with Don Light, where he continued to
book the Oaks as long as they were in gospel music.

Bobby Clark, Tenor

Replaced Hobart Evans, mid-1957; left in late 1957
when the Oaks returned to semi-professional status.

Tommy Fairchild, Pianist

Replaced Powell Hassell, late 1957; sang lead for
several months until Willie Wynn joined; left in
1960 but returned in 1961; left in early 1972 to join
the Blackwood Brothers. Was the last band
member to be a partner in the Oak Ridge Boys.

Willie Wynn, Tenor

From Moultrie, Georgia, where he was a member
of the FFA Quartet. Joined ORQ in 1958; resigned

in 1972. Sang with the Statesmen; later formed his
own group, the Tennesseans; now singing with a
country group, Sweetwater.

Gary Trusler, Pianist

Replaced Tommy Fairchild in 1960.

James Goss, Pianist

Replaced Gary Trusler in 1960; left in the same
year and was replaced by Tommy Fairchild. Later
died in a plane crash.

Gary McSpadden, Baritone

Replaced Ronnie Page in 1962; left in 1964; became
a member of the Bill Gaither Trio, New Gaither
Vocal Band, and a solo gospel artist.

Jim Hammill, Baritone

Replaced Gary McSpadden in 1964; left at the end
of 1964; joined the Rebels; later joined the
Kingsmen.

Bill (later William Lee) Golden, Baritone

From Brewton, Alabama, where he was a member
of the Pilots Trio. Joined ORB in early 1965.

Duane Allen, Lead

From Taylortown, Texas. Former member of the
Prophets. Joined ORB in May 1966.

Noel Fox, Bass

From Columbia, Tennessee. Formerly with the Tennesseans and the Harvesters. Replaced Herman Harper in 1968; left in 1972 to work for Don Light Talent; later booked for the Jim Halsey Agency; left to become the general manager of the Oaks' publishing companies, Silverline and Goldline.

Richard Sterban, Bass

From Camden, New Jersey. Former member of the Keystones and the Stamps; replaced Noel Fox in 1972.

Joe Bonsall, Tenor

From Philadelphia, Pennsylvania. Former member of the Faith Four and the Keystones. Replaced Willie Wynn in 1973.

The Oak Ridge Boys Band

Greg Gordon, Drums, Bass

Played drums 1965–69, later bass (1970–71). Filled in on vocals for both Duane and William Lee. Founding member of the Boys Band. Now sings on sessions in Nashville.

"Little David" Smith, Guitar

Late sixties. Now a solo gospel artist.

Mark Ellerbee, Drums

1970-1980. Now counseling Vietnam veterans and playing in local bands in Tallahassee, Florida.

Don Breland, Bass

1971 to present.

Tony Brown, Pianist

Replaced Tommy Fairchild, 1972; left in 1974.
Played with Elvis Presley; later toured with
Emmylou Harris and Rodney Crowell/Rosanne
Cash. Now vice president a&r of MCA Records
Nashville.

John Rich, Guitarist

Joined in 1972; left in 1974.

Garland Craft, Pianist

Former member of the Keystones. Replaced Tony
Brown in 1974; left to form Cedar Creek in 1980.
Toured with country singer T. Graham Brown in
1986.

B. James Lowery, Guitarist

Replaced John Rich in 1974; left in 1976 to join
Larry Gatlin's band; founding member of the Boys
Band; now a Nashville session musician and a
member of the Jimmy Hall Band.

Rusty Golden, Keyboards and Percussion

1976-77. Son of group member William Lee Golden;
left to form the Boys Band; later, a member of the
Golden Speer group.

Skip Mitchell, Guitarist

1976 to present. Replaced B. Lowery.

Michael Saleem, Drums

1979 to 1980. Played double drums with Mark
Ellerbee until Ellerbee left.

Fred Satterfield, Drums

1980 to present. Replaced Michael Saleem.

Pete Cummings, Guitarist

Joined in 1980; left in 1982.

Ronnie Fairchild, Keyboards

1980 to present. Son of former Oaks pianist Tommy
Fairchild; replaced Garland Craft.

Steve Sanders, Rhythm Guitarist

Former gospel child star Little Stevie Sanders;
founding member of the Boys Band; vocalist for
special Oaks Band project in 1981; full-time
acoustic rhythm guitarist, 1982 to present.

Dewey Dorough, Saxophone and Harmonica

1982 to present.

DISCOGRAPHY

Gospel Albums

From late 1950s to 1973, plus later compilations. In
addition to this selected discography, selections by
the group have appeared on compilations featuring
other artists. Many of these albums are out of print
and complete information, such as label number
and release date, was not always available. The
titles came from historical files. Chart information
data also was not available, since there was rarely
a reliable gospel chart when many of these
recordings were released. Any gospel chart would
not have reflected sales of albums at concerts,
which made up the bulk of many gospel singers'
record sales at this time.

The Oak Ridge Quartet. Cadence CLP 3019.
The Oak Ridge Quartet. Checker LP 10002.
The Oak Ridge Quartet in Concert. Cumberland
　　MGC 29526.
The Oak Ridge Quartet. Sing and Shout. Skylite
　　SRLP 5974.

Wally Fowler and the Oak Ridge Quartet. My God Is Real. Songs of Faith SFLP 100.

The Sensational Oak Ridge Boys from Nashville Tennessee. Starday (also released in Canada on Birchmount BM-783).

Spiritual Jubilee. Accord 7138.

Spiritual Jubilee, Vol. II. Accord SN-7159.

Spiritual Jubilee, Vol. III. "Early Recordings." Accord SN-7199.

The Oak Ridge Boys. Gusto GT 0101.

The Oak Ridge Boys. Gusto/Power Pak PG 716.

The Oak Ridge Boys with Sounds of Nashville. Warner Bros. W1497. 1962.

Folk-Minded Spirituals for Spiritual-Minded Folks. Warner Bros. W1521.

Duane Allen Out Front. Heartwarming. 1966.

Songs We Wish We'd Recorded First. Heartwarming HWM 1901.

It's Happening. Heartwarming.

New Horizons. Heartwarming HWS 1988.

Thanks! Heartwarming HWS 3036.

Talk About the Good Times. Heartwarming HWS 3068.

International. Heartwarming HWS 3091. (Vista R1716).

Performance: The Oak Ridge Boys "Live." Heartwarming HWS 3118.

Light. Heartwarming.

Street Gospel. Heartwarming R3200.

Super Gospel. Heartwarming. R3320. 1974.

Gospel Gold. Heartwarming.

I Know. Vista.

Jesus Christ. Vista.

Sing Their Favorites. Vista.

Oak Ridge Boys' Greatest Hits. Hansen MM 125.

A Higher Power. Nashville NLP 2086.

Gospel, Vol. I. Out of Town OTD 8017.

Gospel, Vol. II. Out of Town OTD 8023.

Sing Super Gospel Hits, Vol. I. Skylite SLP-6091.
Sing Super Gospel Hits, Vol. II. Skylite SLP-6093.
Live. Rockland Road RR106. 1977.
Sensational. Starday SLP 356.
Hymns. The Oaks ORB 1111. 1973.
Country Gospel.
Less of Me.
Go Out to the Program.
At Their Best. Liberty. LN 10046. 1980.

Albums by The Oak Ridge Boys Band

Recorded without the singers. These are custom
recordings.

Rockland Road. Rockland Road RR-101. 1974.
Planet Time. (Released under the band name
    Rockland Road.) Signatur (Sweden) SILP 6044.
    1977.
Super Hits. The Oaks (label) ORB 2222.
The Top 10 by The Top 4. Superior S-1005.
Tarzan. (Solo album by Tony Brown.)

Gospel Albums by The Oak Ridge Boys

For Columbia Records 1973–76, including later
compilations. These recordings were designed to
broaden the Oaks' following in country music and
preceded their breakthrough recordings for ABC/
Dot, now MCA.

The Oak Ridge Boys. Columbia KC 32742.
Sky High. Columbia KC 33057.
*Old Fashioned, Down Home, Hand Clappin', Foot
    Stompin', Southern Style, Gospel Quartet Music.*
    Columbia KC 33935.
Best of the Oak Ridge Boys. Columbia KC 35302.

All Our Favorite Songs (sepia-tone cover picture).
CBS 81896.
All Our Favorite Songs (multi-photo cover). CBS
FC 37737.
Smoky Mountain Gospel. Priority (Columbia's now
defunct gospel label) PC 38467.

Oak Ridge Boys Albums for MCA Records (formerly ABC/Dot)

The Oaks' found major pop and country success
with their recordings for MCA. This list includes
release date, highest position on *Billboard*'s country
album charts and RIAA sales certification (500,000
for gold, 1 million for platinum).

Y'all Come Back Saloon. Dot/ABC DO-2093. 9/77.
No. 8. Gold.
Room Service. ABC AY 1065. 5/78. No. 3. Gold.
The Oak Ridge Boys Have Arrived. ABC AY 1135.
3/79. No. 5. Gold.
Together. MCA 3220. 3/80. No. 10. Gold.
Greatest Hits. MCA 5150. 10/80. No. 5. Platinum.
Fancy Free. MCA 5209. 5/81. No. 1. Platinum.
Bobbie Sue. MCA 5294. 2/82. No. 1. Gold.
Oak Ridge Boys Christmas. MCA 5365. 9/82. No. 9.
Gold.
American Made. MCA 5390. 1/83. No. 2. Gold.
Deliver. MCA 5455. 10/83. No. 6. Gold.
Greatest Hits II. MCA 5496. 8/84. No. 2. Gold.
Step on Out. MCA 5555. 3/85. No. 3.
Seasons. MCA 5714. 3/86. No. 8.
American Harmony. Heartland Music H 1031. 5/86.
A compilation of MCA hits marketed on
television only.
Christmas Again. MCA 5799. 9/86
When the Fast Lane Ends. MCA 5945 2/87.

William Lee Golden

American Vagabond. MCA 5749. 6/86.

The Oak Ridge Boys Singles on Columbia

These are the singles that reached the *Billboard* country charts and their highest position. Singles by gospel music record companies were released to radio stations only. The gospel industry generally is not a singles oriented industry.

Family Reunion. 6/76. No. 83.
Rhythm Guitar. 6/79. No. 94.

The Oak Ridge Boys Singles on MCA

Includes release date, highest position reached on *Billboard*'s country singles chart and RIAA sales certification (1 million for gold, 2 million for platinum).

"Y'all Come Back Saloon," 6/77. No. 3.
"You're the One," 11/77. No. 2.
"I'll Be True to You," 2/78. No. 1.
"Cryin' Again," 8/78. No. 3.
"Come on In," 11/78. No. 3.
"Sail Away," 3/79. No. 2.
"Dream On," 8/79. No. 7.
"Leaving Louisiana," 11/79. No. 1.
"Trying to Love Two Women," 3/80. No. 1.
"Heart of Mine," 6/80. No. 3.
"Beautiful You," 12/80. No. 3.
"Elvira," 3/81. No. 1. Platinum.
"I'm Settin' Fancy Free," 8/81. No. 1.
"Bobbie Sue," 1/82. No. 1. Gold.
"So Fine," 5/82. No. 22.
"I Wish You Could Have Turned My Head," 7/82. No. 2.

"Thank God for Kids," 10/82. No. 3.
"American Made," 2/83. No. 1.
"Love Song," 5/83. No. 1.
"Ozark Mountain Jubilee," 10/83. No. 5.
"I Guess It Never Hurts to Hurt Sometimes," 2/84.
    No. 1.
"Everyday," 7/84. No. 1.
"Make My Life With You," 11/84. No. 1.
"Little Things," 3/85. No. 1.
"Touch a Hand, Make a Friend," 7/85. No. 1.
"Come on In (You Did the Best That You Could
    Do)," 10/85. No. 3.
"Juliet," 3/86. No. 15.
"You Made a Rock of a Rolling Stone," 6/86. No. 24.

William Lee Golden Singles

"Love Is The Only Way Out," 6/86.
"You Can't Take It With You," 10/86.

Oak Ridge Boys Guest Vocals on Other Artists' Recordings

This is a selected discography of guest vocal
appearances by the Oaks.

*My Head Hurts, My Feet Stink, and I Don't Love
    Jesus.* Jimmy Buffett. MCA.
Loves Me Like a Rock. Paul Simon. Columbia.
Same Ole Me. George Jones. Epic.
When You Get To The Heart. Barbara Mandrell.
    MCA.
Or What. Junior Farrington, Jr. Dog.
Out Goin' Cattin'. Sawyer Brown. Joe Bonsall, guest
    vocalist. EMI America.

MAJOR AWARDS

Dove Awards

Album of the Year. *It's Happening* 1969.
Best Male Group. 1970.
Best Male Group. 1972.
Best Instrumentalist. Pianist Tony Brown. 1972.
Best Album. *Light* 1972.
Best Liner Notes. *Light* 1972.
Best Album Cover. *Light* 1972.
Best Album. *Street Gospel* 1973.
Best Album Cover. *Street Gospel* 1973.
Best Album Photography. *Street Gospel* 1973.

Dove Awards for Song of the Year (presented to the songwriter) for Oak Ridge Boys singles:

"Jesus Is Coming Soon," 1969.
"Because He Lives," 1974.

Grammy Awards

Best Gospel Performance. "Talk About the Good Times" 1971.

Best Gospel Performance. "The Baptism of Jesse
Taylor" 1974.
Best Traditional Gospel Performance. "Where the
Soul Never Dies" 1976.
Best Traditional Gospel Performance. "Just a Little
Talk With Jesus" 1977.
Best Vocal Performance by a Country Group or
Duo. "Elvira" 1982.

Country Music Association Awards

Vocal Group of the Year. 1978.
Instrumental Group of the Year. The Oaks Band.
1978.
Single of the Year. "Elvira" 1981.
Instrumental Group of the Year. The Oaks Band.
1986.

Academy of Country Music Awards

Best Vocal Group. 1977.
Best Vocal Group. 1979.
Best Album. *Y'all Come Back Saloon* 1979.
Single of the Year. "Elvira" 1982.

Music City News Awards

Band of the Year. The Oaks Band. 1978.
Best Single of the Year. "Elvira" 1982.

American Music Awards

Best Country Group of the Year. 1982.
Best Country Video. *Everyday.* 1985.

Billboard Magazine Awards

Breakthrough Award. 1977.

Number One Country Group. 1978.
Number One Country Group, Singles. 1980.
Number One Country Group, Albums. 1980.
Number One Country Group. 1980.
Bill Williams Memorial Award. 1981.

Cashbox Magazine Awards

Country Vocal Group, Singles. 1978.
Country Vocal Group, Singles. 1979.
Country Vocal Group, Albums. 1979.
Country Vocal Group, Singles. 1980.
Country Vocal Group, Albums. 1981.
Country Crossover Group Pop, Singles. 1981.
Country Crossover Group Pop, Albums. 1981.
Country Vocal Group, Singles. 1983.

Record World Magazine Awards

Country Singles Award. 1977.
Country Vocal Group, Singles. 1978.
Country Vocal Group, Albums. 1978.
Country Vocal Group, Singles. 1979.
Country Vocal Group, Albums. 1980.
Country Vocal Group, Albums. 1981.
Most Promising Male Group, Albums. 1981.
Top Country Crossover Group. 1981.

Radio and Records Country Music Poll

Country Group of the Year. 1978–80.
Single of the Year. "Elvira" 1981.

Performance Readers' Poll

Country Act of the Year. 1981.

Country Rhythms International Fan Awards

Best Country Group. 1982.

Kountry Korral Magazine (Sweden) Awards

Number One Country Group. 1975.
Number One Gospel Group. 1975.

Juke Box Operators of America Awards

Country Group of the Year. 1980.
Song of the Year. "Elvira" 1981.

Disc Jockey Awards

Group of the Year in Country. 1980.

Radio Programmers Choice Awards

Vocal Group of the Year. 1981.

Broadcast Music Inc. (BMI) Awards

Most Performed Song of the Year. "Elvira" 1981.

Billboard/Wembley Festival of Country Music Awards

Best Country Group. 1975.

American Guild of Variety Artists Awards

Best Country Vocal Group of the Year. 1981.

National Association for Campus Activities Awards

Best Major Country Performance. 1983, 1985, 1986.

INDEX